TALES OF THE
POSSESSED

TALES OF THE
POSSESSED

EXTRAORDINARY TRUE LIFE EXPERIENCES

C. TORRINGTON

ARCTURUS

ARCTURUS

This edition published in 2017 by Arcturus Publishing Limited
26/27 Bickels Yard, 151–153 Bermondsey Street,
London SE1 3HA

ISBN: 978-1-78599-381-7
DA004685UK

Printed in China

Contents

A DIABOLICAL BUSINESS

'It was a very extraordinary spectacle for those of us who were present to see this wicked spirit express himself through the mouth of the poor woman and to hear now the sound of a masculine voice, now that of a feminine one, but so distinct the one from the other that we would not believe that the woman alone spoke but thought we heard two people in a lively quarrel loading one another with abuse. And in effect there were two persons, there were two different wills – on one side the demon who wished to break the body of which he was in possession, and on the other the woman who wished to be delivered from the enemy who possessed her.'

(Einhard, *Translation of the Blessed Martyrs of Christ, Saints Marcellinus and Petrus*, 830, English translation by T. K. Österreich)

The scholar and scribe Einhard (c.775–84) at work.

DEMONS: METAPHORICAL AND REAL

In 2015, a British court sentenced John Thomson-Glover to three years in prison for hiding cameras in a school to film pupils when they were undressed. The judge described him as 'essentially a good man, brought low by the demons that possess him'. Of course the judge did not mean that Thomson-Glover was literally a victim of demonic possession and, if he had been, the accused should not have been held responsible for his actions.

Demonic possession is often used metaphorically like this – indeed, we are more likely to encounter the idea in this sort of context than in any other. Yet the potency of the expression relies on the long tradition of belief in actual demonic possession. The phenomenon can be traced through history and around the world, and for many religious groups today the idea of demonic possession, as a literal and terrifying event, is very much alive. It has changed little over the centuries, as we shall see from the stories which follow.

A FAMILIAR PATTERN

If Thomson-Glover had been possessed by demons, he would have been expected to be writhing on the floor, swearing obscenely, and speaking in a strange voice. He would not have been meticulously drilling holes in walls to spy on children as they showered. The description above given by Einhard, an intellectual working in the court of the Holy Roman Emperor Charlemagne in the ninth century, is far more typical of what we would expect of a possessed individual.

Possession generally involves bizarre physical contortions and changed voices, as also described by Einhard. The possessed might harm themselves or others, utter blasphemies and speak or act in licentious, flagrantly sexual ways. They show disgust or terror at the presence of holy or sacred objects. They often reveal hidden knowledge (gnosis), speak languages they do not know, and might have wounds such as scratches and bite-marks that appear without visible cause.

PAST AND PRESENT

The idea of people possessed by evil spirits against their will is at least as old as the Babylonian and ancient Assyrian cultures. Often there is thought to be a special way a person has become possessed. It might be the result of a curse cast on them by a sorcerer, or some unfortunate mishap such as stepping over a dead body. Or the demons can have been invited, in a Satanic ritual. More often, at least in recent Christian tradition, there is no initiating moment that can be identified – they just find their way in, like disease.

Indeed, the earliest accounts of possession by evil

spirits are often just descriptions of illness that people assumed to be caused by spirits because they knew of no other cause. We shall not deal here with these accounts that use demons as scapegoats for regular types of illness. Instead, we shall focus on some of the well-documented instances of possession of the type that Einhard describes.

SPIRITS INVITED AND INVADING

In many societies, shamanic ritual and religious ecstasy play an important part in spiritual life. Shamans are individuals with a special role in a community. Considered emissaries or messengers between the human and spirit realms, they can travel or provide a conduit between the two by going into a trance or state of ecstasy, a type of altered consciousness. The physical signs associated with shamanistic ecstasy are remarkably similar to those of demonic possession. It appears that there is a state that some people can enter, often at will, in which they might 'speak in tongues' (called *glossolalia*), move energetically, contort their bodies and enter a different state of consciousness.

> **GLOSSOLALIA**
> 'Speaking in tongues' is associated not only with shamanistic rituals but with some forms of Christian worship, such as spirit baptism in the

*Shaman in Ecuadorian Amazonia during a
ceremony that uses the psychotropic brew ayahuasca.*

Pentecostal Church. Formally known as glossolalia, speaking in tongues has the same sound patterns wherever it is found in the world and seems to come from deep brain structures, independent of learned languages (taking a neurological perspective), or from a universal method of communicating with the spirit world (from a supernatural perspective).

These rituals differ from the type of possession we shall be concerned with in that the spirits have been invited to enter the host and will be dismissed at the end of the ritual. The human host remains in overall control and makes use of the spirits. The same is true of mediums who claim to contact or channel the spirits of the dead. On the contrary, in cases of possession the spirit usually comes uninvited and refuses to leave. Forcing an uninvited spirit to vacate a possessed person is extremely difficult.

VIKING BERSERKERS

The state of frenzy that plagues the possessed and is the stock-in-trade of the shaman has been put to less spiritual use in the past. The Viking raiders often entered a state of fury called *berserkergang* ('going berserk') in the heat of battle or during arduous work. It enabled them to perform tasks which seemed beyond human power. Its onset was marked by shivering, teeth-chattering and chills, followed by the face swelling and changing colour. The berserkers flew into a great rage, howling like wild animals, biting the edges of their shields, and slashing at everyone and everything they met with no distinction between friend and foe. At the end of the fury, the berserker fell into a lethargy, remaining numb and feeble, which could last for a day more – all very much like the state of possession.

LETTING THE DEMONS IN . . .

Societies that make a habit of using shamanistic ecstasy or other forms of altered consciousness usually have rituals which help to lead people into the altered state. These might involve chanting, rhythmical music, rituals for cleansing (bathing, fasting, chastity), wearing special costumes, eating particular foods and sometimes using drugs to produce hallucinations. These preparations can be seen as opening a door that allows the person's mind to be taken over, either by an aspect of themselves or by a spirit from within or outside themselves – however we care to interpret it. The affected person might consider themselves to be absent, and another spirit to have taken over their body. Or they might see themselves to be used as a conduit through which a spirit can speak and act, with

Hereward, the Saxon hero, famously turned into a berserker. Dressed in only a silk shirt and hose, he urges his men to join him against the Normans invading Britain.

them taking a back seat while it happens. 'Possession' is an aggressive act, whereas acting as a conduit might be cooperative. The range of activities the 'other' might engage in can range from the benign and revelatory (bestowing the rules of a divinity, showing a vision of paradise) to the hostile and destructive (committing acts of violence or desecration, for instance). There are two recognized states: the person may be lucid, aware of what is going on and able to remember it later, or they may be unconscious. In most of the possession cases we shall discuss later, possession takes over completely and the victim is unconscious – often with their eyes closed – during the bouts of spirit activity.

When the ritual is over, the person communicating with or channelling spirits has a way of dismissing them and taking back full control of their own body. This is not the case for the possessed individual, who is sometimes never rid of their demons.

AUTOMATIC WRITING

Pearl Curran, a housewife living in St Louis, Missouri, soared to fame in the second decade of the 20th century as the amanuensis of 'Patience Worth', a writer who had supposedly died in the 17th century. Patience, the story goes, was a single Englishwoman who had emigrated to Nantucket Island in the 1600s and been killed in an Indian raid. Curran used a Ouija board to

Pearl Curran used a Ouija board to channel the spirit of long-deceased writer Patience Worth.

channel the spirit of Patience, who wrote accomplished poetry and novels. Her work was dictated to Curran at considerable speed, but needed no revision. Her poetry and prose reveal considerable knowledge of the plants, customs and clothing of the time, and of many other times. As Pearl was relatively uneducated, it was easy for people to be persuaded that she could not be composing the works herself.

IN OR ON?

In Western tradition, demons or spirits are often seen as inhabiting the body, taking it over by entering into it. In the Haitian Vodun (or Voodoo) tradition, the possessing spirit, or *loa*, is considered instead to ride on the priest or priestess, who is called the 'horse'. In weekly Saturday rituals, Vodun practitioners call *loa* to appear. The *loa* can be boisterous or even violent, leading the 'horse' to thrash and flail about or convulse. The individual's behaviour during possession reflects the character of the *loa* – so, for example, someone possessed by a snake-like spirit might writhe on the floor. Once the particular *loa* is recognized – through it identifying itself, or from the style of its riding – appropriate props and offerings are brought to it. At the end of the ceremony, control is returned to the individual and the *loa* leaves.

Haitian Ounsis (vodun priestesses) threw goat and chicken blood on their white robes during the Dahomey rite on 2ᵈ April 2011 in Souvenance, Haiti.

Occasionally a *loa* comes unbidden and takes over a person involuntarily. This can be difficult to dismiss. A person can also be saddled with a spirit if they have been cursed. This is possession in the normal sense, and requires a complex exorcism by an experienced sorcerer.

DRIVING THE DEMONS OUT

While voluntary or benign accommodation of a spirit might be dispelled with the end of a ritual, or with simple words or rituals of dismissal, possession is beyond such straightforward control. The only way to cure a person who is possessed by demons or spirits is through exorcism. It is an often prolonged and possibly violent ritual, especially if the demon puts up a fight.

Exorcism follows a similar pattern even between widely different cultures. It is generally a special ritual involving holy or magical objects, demanding the demon or spirit identify itself, and commanding it to leave. Forcing the demon to give its name is a key feature that we see again and again in Christian, Vodun and Japanese rituals of exorcism.

The process imposes rigorous trials on the exorcist, such as fasting, and extended periods of prayer or struggle. Demons are generally at their most violent and offensive during an exorcism. They resent the intervention of the exorcist and battle to retain control of the possessed individual. The struggle becomes increasingly violent and can put the life of the victim in peril, and sometimes even that of the exorcist. We shall see many attempts at driving out evil spirits in the following stories of possession, some successful and some not.

Christian exorcisms generally follow the pattern laid out in the *Rituale Romanum*, a volume which brought together many of the church's holy rituals in 1614. Exorcism is a ritual, not a rite, so does not have to follow precise wording but can be varied according to circumstances. The priests performing exorcism are forbidden from engaging in discussion or debate with the demons, and must trust nothing they say. Since demons are great deceivers, they are likely to draw even the most virtuous person into heresy or error if their arguments are entertained.

FAKING IT?

There have been many attempts to give rational explanations for both demonic possession and religious or ritual ecstasy. The most common charges are that the individuals are either faking their affliction (role-playing in the case of shamans) or are mentally ill.

Faking possession would certainly be a grand,

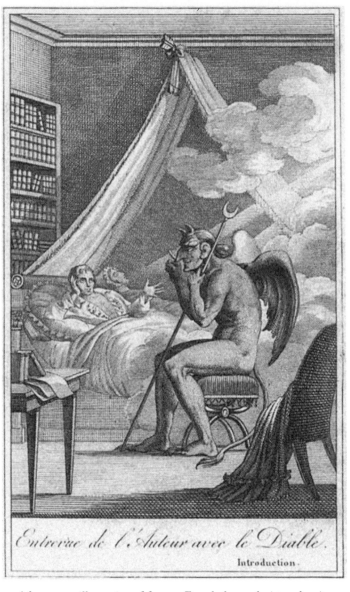

Entrevue de l'Auteur avec le Diable.

Introduction.

A humorous illustration of famous French demonologist and writer
Jacques Albin Simon Collin de Plancy from 1825. De Plancy is having
a friendly exchange with the devil while reclining in bed.

attention-seeking gesture. It's impossible to rule out some fakery, yet it seems unlikely that all recorded instances have been faked. There are too many similarities between instances in cultures widely spread through time and geographical space for that to be plausible. The quite astonishing physical feats achieved by some people while in a state of trance or possession make faking seem virtually impossible. Although it is well known that in certain circumstances people can show incredible strength or endurance, this can't generally be called up at will. Further, the experience for most possessed individuals is far too unpleasant for deliberately faking it to appeal to any but the most disturbed individuals.

This type of rationalization only moves the mystery back a step, in any case. If someone is faking, they have to be faking something specific. You can dress up as a policeman and pretend to be one, but only because there actually are policemen. Pretending to be possessed only works if we all acknowledge there is something to pretend. Even if we don't believe in either possession or demons, there has to be some agreement of what the faking or role-playing is emulating. And why, if rooted in nothing, is it always the same, from 12th-century Norfolk to 21st-century Haiti? There may not be demons, but there is something going on.

SICK OR SANE?

The symptoms of possession are superficially similar to those of some recognized medical conditions, such as epilepsy, and some forms of mental illness. Today, members of the Christian churches who are considering exorcism must carry out rigorous checks to ensure that the victim is not ill rather than possessed. The church, at least, sees that there is room for confusion and is acting to avoid terrible errors, such as have happened in the past.

Mental illness does not explain shamanism. It is not credible that every society that has shamanic rituals coincidentally has a person with just the right type of psychotic disturbance available whenever a new shaman is needed. It is far more likely that all – or at least many – people have the potential to enter such an altered state. Indeed, in some cultures, a rite of passage which involves entering an altered state of consciousness is a necessary step on the path to adulthood. And although a shaman or religious leader might lead or initiate celebrations, typically many or all of the group will engage to some degree. This leads to the suspicion that whatever is going on in the mind of the possessed person is something that could afflict any (or many) of us.

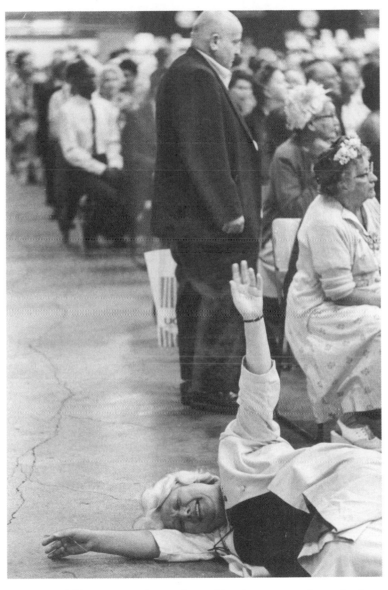

Pentecostal Christians are known for speaking in tongues and experiencing transcendental moments of religious ecstasy. Here, a worshipper in Canada has achieved an altered state of consciousness resulting in prostration.

DISSOCIATIVE IDENTITY DISORDER (DID)

There is one condition recognized by psychology that has many similarities with the presentation of possession. This is the relatively rare psychiatric condition called Dissociative Identity Disorder (DID, previously known as Multiple Personality Disorder, or MPD). A person with DID manifests one or more alternate personalities which take over their mind and body at different times. They often undergo physically strenuous transition events, characterized by blinding headaches, changing facial expressions, sometimes extreme muscle tightening, perspiration and so on. Not only are there considerable differences between the personalities that might inhabit one body, but often there are physical differences, too. They might be of different gender. Some physiological symptoms, such as digestive problems, allergies or susceptibility to certain drugs, might manifest in only one personality and leave another unaffected. The American psychologist Corbett Thigpen reported treating a DID-afflicted woman, 'Eve' (real name Chris Costner Sizemore), who in one persona was allergic to nylon but in her everyday persona was not.

A person with DID is not generally aware that they share their mind and body with other personalities. The transition is not brought about deliberately, as is the case with spiritual ecstasy encouraged by ritual acts.

Actress Joanne Woodward portrays one of the personalities of 'Eve' in The Three Faces of Eve, *1957.*

Nor can it be neatly ended by another ritual act, a command, or the removal of some stimulus that kept it going (such as rhythmic drumming). It is, like demonic possession, unwilled and unwanted. It is this distinction – that there is no control – that marks the person with DID a patient and the person possessed by demons a victim.

We don't understand how DID comes about. One model of explanation is that we all have a sort of mind-map which forms personality, but that a different mind-map could coexist defining a different personality. Something can trigger a switch between the two.

JEKYLL AND HYDE

The novella *The Strange Case of Dr Jeykyll and Mr Hyde*, published by Robert Louis Stevenson in 1886, could describe a classic case of either DID or demonic possession. The fictional Jekyll has found a potion which allows him to split his personality. Drinking the potion causes physical changes, including painful contortions, ending with him having a different physical appearance as well as different behaviour. Jekyll's alter ego, Mr Hyde, is selfish, seeks only sensation, and acts violently. The appearance of Hyde initially depends on Jekyll seeking to take the potion – just as shamans are inhabited by a spirit only after an established ritual. After a while, though, Hyde appears spontaneously, as do the alter egos of those with DID or possessed by demons. Ultimately, Jekyll is not able to banish Hyde, even with the use of his potion.

Stevenson was writing long before DID was recognized as a psychological condition, and before anthropological work on possession and shamanic rituals was widely known.

STILL GOING STRONG

Although some stories of possession are very old, some are recent. Possession, or a belief in possession, is not merely a fringe concern of non-mainstream religions. Pope Benedict XVI (2005–2013) surprised some followers by announcing that the Devil is very much a force for evil in the 21st century, a view many Christians see as old-fashioned. Exorcism is on the rise in the Catholic Church. The Italian Association of Psychiatrists and Psychologists claims that half a million Italians seek exorcism each year. The International Association of Exorcists (IAE) was founded in 1990 by six priests, including Fr Gabriele Amorth (1925–2016), who reportedly performed 160,000 exorcisms and was endorsed by the Vatican. IAE has several hundred members worldwide, but finds it difficult to recruit new approved exorcists. The job is considered too scary for young priests to take on. In the USA, the term 'deliverance' has gained ground, and is increasingly popular. Deliverance has even become a sub-category of self-help, with abundant advice on casting out demons of all types without the help of a religious guide.

> 'Once you hear a Satanic growl, you never forget it. It's like smelling Margherita pizza for the first time. It's something you never forget.'
>
> Rev. Gabriele Amorth

WITCHES, GHOSTS, POLTERGEISTS AND DEMONS

The taxonomy of evil spirits is complex. On the simplest level, though, there are considerable differences between witches, ghosts, poltergeists and demons.

Witches

Witchcraft is not the same thing as being possessed by demons, but demonic possession is often associated with historic cases of alleged witchcraft. Witches, according to Pope Eugenius IV in 1437, are those who have made a contract with the Devil, in exchange for which they are given power to do evil by commanding demons. Far from being possessed, witches are in the enviable position of having demons do their bidding. When we see demonic possession in accounts of witchcraft, it is not generally the witch who is claimed to be possessed by demons, but the witch's victims.

This was the case in three very famous examples from France during the 1600s – the possessions in Aix, Loudun and Lanviers. In each instance, young nuns claimed to have been possessed by demons following the evil influence of some charismatic priest.

Ghosts

There is less of a link between demons and ghosts. Occasionally, a case of possession will seem to involve the person being possessed by the ghost of a dead person, but this is relatively infrequent. One example is the American woman Anna Ecklund, who seems to have been possessed not only by regular demons but also by the spirits of her dead uncle and his mistress. Another is the possession of survivors of the Japanese tsunami by spirits of some of the victims. In Vodun, it is the spirits of the dead (Guédé) who possess a cursed person. But these are atypical; it is more common for people to be plagued and harassed by ghosts than to be possessed by them.

Poltergeists

Poltergeist activity can look very like demonic possession and there is a clear link here. A poltergeist (or 'noisy ghost', from the German), typically causes objects to move or fly around, unexplained noises such as scratching, bangs, and crashes, the disappearance and reappearance of objects, and inexplicable damage.

Poltergeist activity is most often associated with teenagers and disturbed or unhappy children.

In 1599, the Jesuit Martin Delrio wrote *Disquisitionum magicarum libri sex* (Six Books of Magical Investigations), in which he described eighteen kinds of demons or demonic apparitions. The sixteenth type included 'spectres which in certain times and places or homes are wont to occasion various commotions and annoyances' and which might keep someone awake by 'clattering of pots and hurling of stones, and, having pulled away his mattress, turned him out of his bed'.

This sounds very like a poltergeist. The 'turning out' of bed recalls the many accounts of beds moving vigorously in possession cases – it is a recurring theme, as we shall see. The tradition of poltergeist-like activity is very old. The Ancient Assyrians had a tradition of ekimmu, which were the spirits of those who died violently or suddenly and lacked a proper burial. The ekimmu visited households at night, causing disruption and chaos – they could even kill the members of the household and could take possession of people.

FROM INFESTATION TO POSSESSION
The process of possession was sometimes divided into the following categories:

• Infestation – strange and troubling phenomena affect an area (such as a house) rather than being

---

restricted to a specific person. This is what we associate with poltergeists

• Obsession – a person is the victim of irrational and oppressive or obsessive thoughts, including thoughts of suicide or violence towards others, but does not lose consciousness or control (this is similar to the clinical definition of OCD, Obsessive Compulsive Disorder)

• Oppression – demons make physical assaults on a person, leaving visible wounds or marks

• Possession – a person is forcibly taken over by a supernatural entity, which can speak and act through them.

Demons

In Christian mythology, demons are the fallen angels who rebelled against God and were cast out of Heaven alongside their leader, Lucifer. Lucifer (or Satan) is chief of demons, and is also known simply as the Devil. Beelzebub is his right-hand demon. Then there are hordes of lesser demons, only some of which are ever named. The aim of the Devil, and the demons in his train, is to trap souls, betraying people into damnation. The possessed individual is in dire danger of having his or her soul snatched by the Devil – this is what the exorcist must battle against. It is a perilous undertaking.

THE LAMENT OF THE POSSESSED

Exorcists are themselves subject to assault by demons, and many fall prey to possession through their work. Father Surin, who was involved in the Loudun possession, suffered from harassment by demons for decades afterwards. He described how he felt himself turning into a demon. When he tried to make the sign of the cross, 'the other soul turns my hand aside, or takes the finger between the teeth and savagely bites it'. He has left a relatively rare first-hand account of being the subject of possession rather than the exorcist or spectator. It is a chilling picture, and nearly 400 years later it is shockingly resonant:

'I find it almost impossible to explain what happens to me during this time, how this alien spirit is united to mine, without depriving me of consciousness or of inner freedom, and yet constituting a second 'me', as though I had two souls . . . I feel as if I had been pierced by the pricks of despair in that alien soul which seems to be mine . . . I even feel that the cries uttered by my mouth come from both souls at once; and I find it hard to determine whether they are the product of joy or frenzy.'

THE DEMONS AND THE POSSESSED

The following stories of demonic possession are taken from different parts of the world and different times, yet there is remarkable similarity between them. They are just a few of the countless examples of such stories. More come to light every year – demonic possession is not a thing of the past. These are some of the more notable and well-known cases and they represent the most common types of possession recorded.

JESUS DRIVES OUT THE DEMONS

In Christianity, stories of possession begin with the Gospels of Mark, Matthew and Luke. They all record an incident when Jesus reportedly drove demons from a man who was so afflicted that he lived in a rocky place among tombs and self-harmed. According to the account, Jesus followed the common model for exorcisms of calling on the demon to say its name and say how many demons were present. The demon replied, 'I am Legion, for we are many.' As Jesus drove the demons out, they begged to be allowed to move into a herd of pigs, exhibiting the usual reluctance of demons to leave the person they have possessed and their fear of expulsion to hell. Demons inhabiting an animal rather than a human is generally classified as infestation, and is certainly an improvement as the demons have taken a step backwards from possession. As it is such an important precedent, the text of this is given here in full:

> 1 They went across the lake to the region of the Gerasenes. 2 When Jesus got out of the boat, a man with an impure spirit came from the tombs to meet him. 3 This man lived in the tombs, and

no one could bind him any more, not even with a chain. 4 For he had often been chained hand and foot, but he tore the chains apart and broke the irons on his feet. No one was strong enough to subdue him. 5 Night and day among the tombs and in the hills he would cry out and cut himself with stones.

6 When he saw Jesus from a distance, he ran and fell on his knees in front of him. 7 He shouted at the top of his voice, 'What do you want with me, Jesus, Son of the Most High God? In God's name don't torture me!' 8 For Jesus had said to him, 'Come out of this man, you impure spirit!'

9 Then Jesus asked him, 'What is your name?'

'My name is Legion,' he replied, 'for we are many.' 10 And he begged Jesus again and again not to send them out of the area.

11 A large herd of pigs was feeding on the nearby hillside. 12 The demons begged Jesus, 'Send us among the pigs, allow us to go into them.' 13 He gave them permission, and the impure spirits came out and went into the pigs. The herd, about two thousand in number, rushed down the steep bank into the lake and were drowned.

14 Those tending the pigs ran off and reported this in the town and countryside, and the people went out to see what had happened. 15 When they came to Jesus, they saw the man who had been possessed by the legion of demons, sitting there, dressed and in his right mind; and they

were afraid. 16 Those who had seen it told the people what had happened to the demon-possessed man – and told about the pigs as well. 17 Then the people began to plead with Jesus to leave their region.

18 As Jesus was getting into the boat, the man who had been demon-possessed begged to go with him. 19 Jesus did not let him, but said, 'Go home to your own people and tell them how much the Lord has done for you, and how he has had mercy on you.' 20 So the man went away and began to tell in the Decapolis how much Jesus had done for him. And all the people were amazed.

Gospel of St Mark, Chapter 5, *Holy Bible*,
New International Version

THE YATTON DAEMONIAC

The unfortunate George Lukins lived in the west of England, in the village of Yatton, Somerset, where he originally worked as a tailor. For eighteen years, apparently starting near Christmas in 1759 or 1760, he suffered terrible fits in which he seemed – and claimed – to be possessed by demons.

By his own account, his troubles began when he had been travelling around the neighbourhood performing in Christmas plays. He suddenly fell senseless to the floor. It took great effort on the part of his companions to rouse him and when he did come round he claimed to have been struck hard by some person – unseen by the others – as punishment for acting in plays. Ever since, he had been subject to terrible fits. Their frequency had increased until by 1778, he was having up to nine fits a day. This prevented him working and so he was poor, malnourished and weak.

Each of his fits followed the same pattern. They began with 'powerful agitation' in his right hand, then his face distorted horribly. He would then begin to shout 'in a roaring voice', claiming to be Satan. The voice called on others in his power – demons – to torment Lukins. Satan commanded the demons to sing, and so Lukins sang. He began with a 'jovial hunting song' in one voice, then switched to a female voice, then sang a pastoral song dialogue in his own voice. After more distortions, the voice of the demon ended with another hunting song in a 'hoarse, frightful voice'. Any episodes in the songs that expressed goodness, innocence or kindness were changed in the demon's song to the opposite meaning.

While Lukins was having a fit, he couldn't bear to hear any good or holy words, but was driven mad by them and responded with shocking blasphemies. After the songs, the demon mocked any attempts Lukins made to avoid his power, threatening to torment him more and more until the end of his life and taunting that no churchman or doctor would be able to save him. The final song was always a corrupted *Te Deum* (a hymn of praise beginning with the words *Te Deum laudamus*, or 'Thee, O God, we praise'). This hymn was sung in two voices, a male and female, but instead of the correct words it was filled with profanities, including many thanks to Satan for giving them power over Lukins.

The possession ended with the demon barking and promoting himself as a splendid demon. Then Lukins made the same vigorous hand gestures as at the start, and finally came to his senses, exhausted and weak.

Sometimes his fits were so violent that someone had to protect Lukins so that he didn't harm himself. Each fit lasted about an hour, and sometimes Lukins would suppose that he turned into some kind of beast, making the noises and actions appropriate to it. His eyes were closed the whole time, but he was conscious of what was going on and could later answer questions about what happened during his fits.

Lukins claimed that he was persecuted by seven demons and they could only be driven out by seven clergymen working together. This was a heavy demand for a small village, and he never managed to rustle up enough clergy to make the attempt. For a long time he was under the care of a surgeon, Mr Smith of Wrington. (At that time, surgeons worked at large, pulling teeth and performing other quick and painful treatments as well as providing medicines and dressing wounds.) Neither Smith nor any of the clergy who attended Lukins could do him any good. He spent 20 weeks in St George's Hospital, where he was declared incurable.

Eventually, in 1778, a Mrs Sarah Barber visited Yatton and encountered Lukins. She had lived in the town previously, and had known him long ago. Remembering that he had always been of good character, she was very concerned to find him having alarming fits, up to nine times a day. She contacted the Rev. Joseph Easterbrook, in Bristol, asking him to help Lukins if he possibly could. Lukins was taken to Bristol, where he continued to have his fits. These made a strong impression on Easterbrook, who was readily convinced they were the effects of evil spirits.

Easterbrook appealed to several clerical colleagues for assistance, approaching those he considered to be 'most cordial in the belief of supernatural influences', but none would become involved. In his own account of the case, Easterbrook names and shames them all. They were: Dr Syraes, Rector of St. Werburgh's; the Rev. Dr Robins, precentor of the cathedral; and the Rev. Mr Brown, rector of Portishead. He then turned to 'certain persons' who were connected to Reverend Wesley – that is, Methodists. They were much more amenable to the idea and a meeting was arranged for 11 a.m. on Friday 13 June, 1788.

The meeting comprised fourteen men in addition to Easterbrook, and quite a number of members of the public who had heard what was going to happen. Although Easterbrook had tried to keep the meeting secret, news of it had got out, and caused quite a stir. Proceedings began with a hymn, which sent Lukins into convulsions, with horrible contortions of the face and the usual vigorous shaking of his right hand. The voice of a demon then spoke through Lukins, mocking Easterbrook for bringing people together for a futile attempt at banishing him from Lukins's body. The demon proclaimed that not only would he never leave, but he would torment Lukins a thousand times more severely on account of the attempt at exorcism.

The demon began to sing, as usual, and to blaspheme. It threatened vengeance on not just Lukins but all who had come to try to drive it out, and then called to its colleague-demons. Adopting a female voice, the demon sang a love-song, and again poured scorn and threats on both Lukins and the attendant clergymen, swearing it would never give up Lukins. He appeared to be in torment, writhing and blaspheming. A different demon seemed to take over, and sang a dialogue in alternating harsh and soft voices, again ending by torturing poor Lukins, so that 'the man was thrown into violent agonies, and blasphemed in a manner too dreadful to be expressed'. The demon then boasted of his power, saying 'I am the great devil', defied the clergy again, and sang a hunting song. At the end of the song, the demon again tormented Lukins, who thrashed and convulsed so vigorously that two strong men could barely hold him down, even though Lukins himself was small and weak. He barked in an 'indescribably horrid' manner, and laughed hideously. The demon then summoned hordes of infernal demons to attend and drive away the clergy. As the churchmen prayed fervently, the demon sang a Te Deum to Satan, singing in different voices, 'We praise thee, O devil; we acknowledge thee to be the supreme governor.'

The noise of the demons grew so loud that the clergy could not continue with their praying and changed instead to singing a hymn. The demonic voices rained curses and threats on them all the while. At last, one of the clergy called upon the demon, in the name of Jehovah, to give its name. It answered simply, 'I am the Devil.' When he then asked why it tormented Lukins, the Devil replied, 'That I may show my power amongst men.' One of the clergymen then asked Lukins to say the name of Jesus, but the response was always 'Devil'.

At last the clergymen seemed to be breaking through the Devil's defences. A small voice from Lukins asked 'Why don't you adjure?' Seeing his advantage, the clergyman demanded the Devil, in the name of the Father, the Son and the Holy Ghost, to depart from the man immediately. The small voice spoke again, saying, 'Must I give up my power?' It was followed by terrible howling, and then another voice, 'Our master has deceived us!' The clergyman continued with his demands that the Devil leave Lukins, and the dialogue of the demons continued:

'Where shall we go?'

'To hell, and return no more to torment this man.'

On this Lukins was wracked with the most terrible

convulsions, and howled even more hideously than before. But this lasted only briefly. Soon he fell still, and said in his own voice, 'Blessed Jesus!' He began to praise God, fell to his knees and recited the Lord's Prayer. He thanked everyone heartily for their help in banishing the Devil, who had tormented him for eighteen years.

A HAITIAN VODUN EXORCISM

Haitian Vodun involves a strong element of spirit possession. The religion fuses elements of spirit beliefs brought by former slaves from West Africa with principles of Christianity imposed on the slave communities by the French in the 18th century. Central to Haitian Vodun are the supreme creator, called Bondye (derived from the French *bon dieu*, or 'good god'), and *loa*, the spirits that act as intermediaries between Bondye and humanity. There are many *loa* that oversee different aspects of life. The *loa* Baron Samedi is leader of the Guédé (or Ghede), the spirits of the dead. He is often called on in cases of possession, since it is the spirits of the dead who are the possessing entities, inflicted on the victim by a sorcerer.

HOW TO CURSE SOMEONE WITH A POSSESSING SPIRIT

Alfred Métraux (see page 48) found the following ritual used to cause possession. The first step is to turn a statue of Saint Expédit upside down, and then say a prayer in front of it. The supplicant promises to have Expédit as his patron if the *lao* will 'Rid me of his head, rid me of his memory, rid me of this thought, rid me of his house.' The

A Vodun believer in front of images honouring Baron Samedi and the Guédé at the National Cemetery of Port au Prince during the celebration of the Day of the Dead.

petitioner then has to strike his machete three times against a stone dedicated to Baron Samedi, uttering the Baron's name. The Baron then possesses him, and speaking through his mouth tells the petitioner to go to the cemetery and make an offering of cut-up bananas and potatoes in front of Baron Samedi's cross. Then he must take a handful of earth for each of the dead he wants to send to the victim and must put them on a path the victim uses. It doesn't matter whether the victim treads in the earth or steps over it; the spirit of the dead will enter him or her at that point. The spirits, once embedded, are fully entangled with the person and very difficult to remove.

The French anthropologist Alfred Métraux, who studied Haitian Vodun in the 1950s, described the exorcism of a man named Antoine, who had previously worked in the docks at Port-au-Prince. Antoine had suddenly fallen ill, and was unable to eat. He lost a lot of weight and could no longer walk. In Haitian society, this was considered a tell-tale sign of possession. The ghosts do not have any special mission, they have no message for the living, they are not trying to seize the possessed person or their soul and take them to hell – they are simply in possession of them because that's what ghosts do. The possessed person becomes very ill and frail, stops eating, spits blood and soon dies. The only remedy is for someone skilled in commanding spirits to drive them out using strong sorcery and rituals.

A first attempt to cure Antoine failed, and finally his family took him to a *mambo*, or Vodun priestess, called Lorgina. Her own *loa*, Brisé, agreed to help. Lorgina detected with the aid of sorcery that Antoine was possessed by three spirits of the dead. As this was a serious case, she had him brought to the house reserved for the spirits of the dead, the Guédé. The Guédé are particularly tricky spirits as they will not always depart when dismissed, but demand another smoke, another drink, and to carry on partying for a while. The priest or priestess has to keep them in check at the same time as making sure they are properly catered for. The Guédé, being already dead, are aware they are beyond harm and so are hard to discipline. They often behave in ostentatiously provocative ways, being loud and sexual, and doing things that would be reckless in a living person, such as eating broken glass or raw chillies.

Lorgina had the signs of the Guédé drawn out on the floor using coffee grounds and ashes, and Antoine's mat placed over the drawing. A table was set for the *loa* Brisé with his special stone, five bunches of leaves and three hollowed-out squashes, called calabashes. Each calabash contained a burning candle, maize and grilled peanuts. Beneath the table were two troughs, filled with a mix of bull's bile, water and plants soaking together.

As Antoine was carried in and placed on his mat, the dead within him constantly berated Lorgina, swearing that she could not drive them out. Antoine was stripped to his underwear and prepared as though he were already a corpse. Following the Haitian tradition, his nostrils were closed with plugs of cotton, his jaw bound with fabric so that it could not open, his arms crossed and his big toes tied together. Lorgina put small piles of peanuts and maize on his chest, palms, forehead and stomach. Then she brought in a hen and rooster and called on the spirits. An assistant took the birds to Antoine and allowed them to peck the food from his body, starting from the head. The rooster refused the food, so another was brought in. After that, one bird was put between Antoine's legs, and the other two on his chest. Lorgina then began to pray, with incantations to the *loa* and to Saint Expédit. She recited many recognizable Catholic prayers and preceded everything by appealing to the three persons of the Christian God.

After praying, Lorgina continued the ritual by passing the hen and two roosters over Antoine's body, starting at his head, while reciting incantations to drive out the evil and allow good into his body. Both Lorgina and her assistant hissed like the snake god Damballah at this point. The assistant repeated the gesture with the fowl, and Antoine began to tremble. Lorgina told him to be still, and invoked her own *loa* and the ancestors and the *loa* of Antoine to save him. One last pass of the chickens, and they were left, confused, by his side. The other items – the calabashes and the stone – were passed over Antoine.

The next stage was more violent, and upsetting for Antoine's relatives. Lorgina began to throw handfuls of the foul mixture from the troughs over him. He trembled and shuddered and tried to get up. She continued with the 'bath' and some of the spectators helped, throwing it over him as he struggled so violently that he threw off his corpse bands. Lorgina said that the bath of rotting leaves and bile was repellent to the dead (and probably unappealing to the living). At last he was exhausted and gave up struggling. Lorgina called to him, saying 'Antoine, Antoine, is it you there?' When he answered with a faint 'yes', her assistant set fire to rum lying around Brisé's stone, scooped up the flames in his hands and scattered them over Antoine's body. Lorgina took the rum in her mouth and spat it over his face. He was restrained when he tried to protect his eyes. At last, an assistant gave Antoine a pummelling massage on his shoulders, inside his elbows, and in the crooks of his knees.

The final part of the ritual took place outside. In

preparation, a trench had been dug and surrounded by three calabashes and seven orange-peel lanterns. Antoine was placed in the trench and given an uprooted banana palm to hold in his arms. Lorgina passed the hen over Antoine, sprinkled him with the contents of the calabashes and intoned a ritual exorcism over him, calling on various saints, *loas*, God and the spirits of the dead. Finally, she poured water over Antoine, then broke the pitcher that had held it, and helped him out of the trench. The hen was not so lucky. She was put into the trench and buried alive, among the roots of the hurriedly planted banana palm. Three still-burning lamps marked the spot.

Antoine was rubbed down with burning rum to complete the driving-out of the dead and then three small charges were let off between his legs. More rum was squirted over him and sprayed to the north, south, east and west while an assistant cracked a special whip. Lorgina then took a white shirt edged with red and burnt a corner of it. Using the blackened part, she drew marks on Antoine's chest and face, then helped him to dress in the shirt. After his feet were washed with water and herbs, he was finally given a cup of tea – which he probably really needed by that stage – and was considered demon-free. The banana palm eventually died, showing that Baron Samedi had accepted the hen buried beneath it as an offering in exchange for saving Antoine. For his part, Antoine was completely healed. He was soon strong enough to return to work in the dockyard.

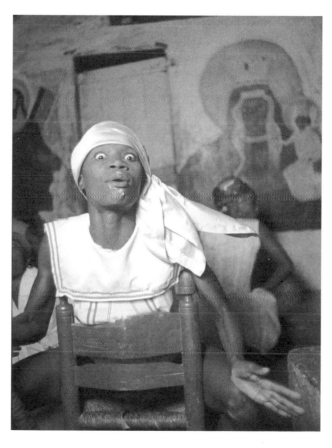

A similar Vodun priestess in Haiti possessed by a god, circa 1980.

ANNELIESE MICHEL

The case of Anneliese Michel, a young university student in Germany, shows what can happen when a belief in possession and exorcism come into conflict with the modern medical and legal systems.

Annaliese had an unusual family background. Her mother had borne an illegitimate daughter in 1948, an act so shameful in rural Bavaria that she had been forced to wear a black veil on her wedding day. Anneliese was born when that child, Martha, was four. Annliese was forced to live devoutly, and when Martha died at the age of eight, the pressure on her increased. The whole family, it seems, had to atone for the mother's 'sin'. Anneliese's devotion ran deep. As a teenager, she slept on a cold stone floor to atone for the sins of the drug addicts sleeping rough at the railway station.

Anneliese's problems began in 1968, when she was sixteen years old. She blacked out at school and the same night had convulsions and bit her tongue. Her fit lasted about a quarter of an hour, and she reported feeling a great weight pinning her down. She had another attack a year later and her mother took her to see a doctor, who ran tests and found no evidence of physical problems but decided to treat her for

Anneliese Michel in good health.

epilepsy. The same autumn Anneliese suffered a series of physical illnesses and ended up at a sanatorium in Bavaria to recover. She had another attack in 1970 and was prescribed anticonvulsant medication. Soon after, she experienced a vision of evil, grimacing, demonic faces. She did not tell anyone about this vision or those that followed.

Dismissed from the sanatorium, Anneliese returned to university but had more convulsions and periods of 'absence' when she seemed to disappear altogether, leaving only an empty, inanimate shell. She suffered a final, major convulsion in June 1972. But other experiences then took the place of the convulsions.

Anneliese's body stiffened periodically, and this increased in frequency. The horrendous faces troubled her almost constantly, she felt an awful sense of dread, and was beset by a terrible stench that no one else could smell. She turned to prayer, becoming ever more fervently religious, but her mother noticed that if she prayed by a statue of the Virgin Mary in their house, her eyes became black and her hands tightened into claws. She visited a shrine to the Virgin in Italy with her father, but was unable to enter it and could not look at an image of Jesus.

The visit to the shrine also prompted the first interaction of the 'demons' with others. On the way home, Anneliese produced a horrible odour – this time others could smell it – and acted violently towards a tour guide who expressed religious views. She also spoke with an altered, masculine-sounding voice. She later said that she was not in control of her actions and felt she was being manipulated by someone or something else.

Anneliese was due to start at college in Würzburg in the autumn of 1973. Her mother took her to the doctor again, and this time she did report the faces that tormented her, calling them devils, and predicted the end of the world in a massive fire that would happen soon. The doctor added to her medication and apparently suggested she see a Jesuit, though he later denied he had done so.

His scepticism had an impact on Anneliese, who began to separate her problems into two camps. She continued to seek medical help for depression, severe headaches and the terrible stench that plagued her, but began to see priests for help with the problems she considered to be spiritual. Some refused to see her, but a young priest from Aschaffenburg, Father Ernst Alt, took an interest in her case and began praying with her. He felt it was a case of demonic possession, but was unable to get the permission that a Catholic priest needed to carry out an exorcism. His assistance helped Anneliese to some degree, and she moved to Würzburg to start her university course.

Once her course started, Anneliese became worse. Prayers with Father Alt and visits to a shrine with a new boyfriend, Peter, helped, but she felt she was increasingly losing control. There were set-backs in her family life: her grandmother died and two of her three sisters moved out of the family home. Her anxiety became more extreme, and she felt she was eternally damned. She had increasingly frequent attacks when she would become stiff, her face transformed into a grimacing mask, and she would scream or cry uncontrollably, and destroy religious objects. She became bed-ridden, unable to eat, move around or sleep.

Annaliese was soon back home, incapable of continuing her studies. Her condition became even worse. She slept at most an hour a night and raged around the house; her body bucked convulsively and went rigid for days on end, and she sprang from kneeling to standing and back so vigorously and often – up to 600 times a day – that her knees became ulcerated and she eventually ruptured the ligaments in them. She would rip off her clothes, violently attack her family, eat spiders, flies and coal, stuff urine-soaked clothes into her mouth, or lick her urine from the floor. Her behaviour was so wild and unnatural that her family was in despair. She seemed to be visited by the spirits of her dead grandmother and sister, and wounds appeared on her hands and feet that her parents interpreted as stigmata (images of the wounds of the crucified Christ).

> **STIGMATA**
>
> The spontaneous appearance of wounds that resemble those of Christ at the crucifixion has been claimed since the Middle Ages. Most often they are puncture wounds in the palms of the hands, as though nails have been driven through the hands. Some stigmatics also have wounds in the feet.

Unable to get hold of Father Alt, the family called on Father Rodewyk, a priest Annaliese had seen previously. When he visited, she was at first in a catatonic state, but roused sufficiently to hold a conversation with him briefly. He asked her name and she responded in a low, unnatural voice, 'Judas.' She appeared coherent and calm for a short period thereafter. He told her he would try to arrange exorcism for her; at that point, when her cramping began again.

Father Rodewyk gained permission from the local bishop for an exorcism, and Father Arnold Renz was appointed to Anneliese's case. As Catholic exorcism is not a rite but a ritual, it does not have to follow a precise form of words or order but can be adapted to the circumstances of the individual. All but the first of Anneliese's exorcisms were recorded on tape, leaving an invaluable record for psychologists, historians and theologians. Father Renz documented the first case in his diary.

The general pattern of a Catholic exorcism is an invocation to God, the angels and saints; extensive praying with the community present (usually the exorcist and family and friends of the afflicted person); sprinkling with holy water or presentation of holy objects; and questioning of the possessing demons. Anneliese responded violently to the holy water, swearing at the priest and demanding he 'stop with that shit'. She had to be held down by three men, and could not endure lying down as she claimed the Devil sat on her back when she did. She responded vigorously and violently throughout the five and a half hours of the ritual, but later said she remembered all of it and wished they had continued as she felt the demons loosening their grip on her.

The exorcism sessions continued over the following weeks. Anneliese was well enough to return to her studies, going home every few days for exorcisms. During these, six demons identified themselves but refused to leave her: Lucifer, Judas Iscariot, Nero, Cain and Adolf Hitler, the latter speaking with appropriate Austrian inflections in his voice. They had detailed and interesting views of the reforms introduced to the Church by the Second Vatican Council (1962–5), which was why Father Renz decided to record the sessions. They also discussed the horrors of Hell. These were considered examples of gnosis – possession of hidden knowledge.

By mid-October 1975, Anneliese's state was improving. She now had positive visitations and revelations from the Virgin Mary and Christ, and the demons were losing some of their power. On the last day of October, a date that had figured often in her revelations and messages, the demons began to leave her, one after another. As each left, she retched violently and vomited. But no sooner were they expelled and everyone was giving thanks than a new demon announced its presence. The demon became increasingly silent, responding less and less in the exorcism sessions. Anneliese became more and more troubled, injuring herself, raging, convulsing and screaming constantly, and eating nothing. She had 67 exorcisms over a period of nine months. But on 1 July 1976, a day on which she had repeatedly predicted that 'all will be well', she died.

Anneliese's parents and two priests were tried for murder. The court found that she had died as a result of having exorcism in place of proper medical attention. Starvation was cited in the autopsy report – she weighed

Father Ernst Alt, Father Arnold Renz and Anneliese Michel's parents on trial for negligent homicide in 1978.

just under 31kg (4st 12lb) at her death, having believed that she could starve the demons out of her system. Her parents and priests were given suspended sentences and probation orders for manslaughter through negligence, allowing her to starve herself to death. In 1999, the Vatican revised the exorcism ritual, the Rituale Romanum, for the first time since 1614, and now insists that all priests permitted to carry out exorcism have medical training.

Annaliese's body has twice been exhumed – once after three years and once after eleven – to confirm that it is actually decaying.

The film *The Exorcism of Emily Rose*, released in 2005, is based on the case of Anneliese Michel. Her mother remains convinced that 'she died to save other lost souls, to atone for their sins'.

THE TRAGIC LIFE OF MARICICA CORNICI

Deep in Communist Romania, in 1982, the infant Maricica Irina Cornici and her brother Vasile were abandoned by their alcoholic mother at the Bârlad Children's Home. Maricica's father had just hanged himself in front of his daughter. The children's home was every bit as bad as the other Romanian orphanages that were exposed to Western scrutiny in the 1990s. While there, Maricica was starved, beaten, and abused. Administrators consistently stole money, food and objects provided to the orphanage for the children, and Maricica and others were used in child pornography as well. At the start of puberty, she hid her emerging sexual characteristics to avoid rape and assault by older boys at the orphanage. She took up karate and became physically aggressive. She also developed an erotic relationship with a close friend in the orphanage, Paraschiva (or Chita) Anghel. This, and a relationship with another girl, had a sadomasochistic element, with Maricica gaining pleasure from hurting her companions. She apparently also heard her father's voice speaking to her during her years at the orphanage. It was hardly an auspicious start in life.

When Maricica left the orphanage in 2001, she

was 19 years old. She settled with what was generously termed a 'foster family' where she worked in exchange for food and lodgings. She also undertook work placements in Germany and saved some money, hoping to move to Germany with Chita. When Maricica later discovered that her foster family had stolen some of her savings, and soon replaced her with another 'daughter' after she left, her distress intensified. She had clearly made more of an emotional investment in them than they did in her.

When Maricica arrived at the Tanacu (Holy Trinity) convent where Chita was living, the girl did not want to go with her. Maricica stayed at the convent, but thwarted in her plan she became increasingly abusive to the nuns, hurling obscene and unfounded anti-gay insults at them. She was also plagued by physical illness. In April 2005 the nuns took her, tied up, to Vaslui County Hospital after a violent, probably suicidal outburst. She was discharged from the psychiatric unit after fifteen days, despite a diagnosis of schizophrenia. Apparently, she had late-stage leukaemia and her death from it would count against the psychiatric unit as a death in their charge.

Back in the convent, she was briefly calm but descended into violence again in May, setting fire to the cell she was living in. Even so, the nuns tried to help her with demonstrations of love, prayers, confession, obedience and fasting. They were unaware of her serious physical condition. But her behaviour and speech led the nuns – who had little or no knowledge of mental illness – to the conviction that she was possessed. It is a suggestion that was possibly first made by a nurse on the psychiatric ward. The priest in charge of the convent, Father Daniel Corogeanu, now considered himself engaged in a war with the Devil.

Long before he encountered Maricica, Corogeanu was already distant from mainstream Western Christianity. At only 29, he was full of crusading passion and commitment, saw himself as a crusader against the Devil, and was already acquiring a cult following far from the very traditional area of Romania where he lived. The Orthodox Church did sanction exorcism, though not in the unconventional form that Father Conrogeanu used. The local people, though, were quite willing to blame all kinds of ills, including simple physical ailments, on demons and exorcism was often more readily available than decent healthcare.

> 'You can't take the Devil out of people with pills.'
> Father Daniel Conrogeanu

The nuns were easily swayed by Father Conrogeanu. Although official policy is that no more than two exorcisms should be carried out on any individual during one year, that three priests should be present, and mental illness must have been ruled out by professionally qualified consultants, Father Conrogeanu took notice of none of this. Under his direction the nuns prepared Maricica for exorcism. They bound her hands and feet and locked her in her cell while they celebrated the Ascension. Later, she was carried into church on a wooden structure that some described as planks with armrests and others said was a crucifix. She was anointed with holy oil on the forehead and wrists. She spent three days in the church. During this time, she ate nothing and possibly drank only holy water. Father Conrogeanu later claimed that she had been offered food and drink but refused it. Her mouth was stopped with a towel to prevent her shouting, cursing and blaspheming while Father Conrogeanu and the nuns prayed for her deliverance from the possessing spirits.

'I consider myself not guilty because [Maricica] Irina Conrici's death was not down to the fact that we kept her locked up.

'We tied her up because she kept hitting and harming herself and we would have found her dead in her room eventually.

'I admit I tied her up and stuck a towel in her mouth and kept her like this for five days.

'I admit that I used to cover her mouth with tape while she took part in daily mass, but only because I did not want her to disturb the service.'

Father Conrogeanu

Afterwards, the nuns returned Maricica to her room and unchained her, but they could not wake her. Although Father Conrogeanu claimed that she was cured, and said that fainting after exorcism was common, the nuns called an ambulance when they found that she had a weak pulse. She was dead on arrival at the hospital. An autopsy found that Maricica died of dehydration, exhaustion and lack of oxygen, but Father Conrogeanu claimed that she died because of an adrenaline shot given in the ambulance (a claim given some credence by a coroner who examined the exhumed body). Father Conrogeanu was sentenced to seven years in prison (and was released in 2011); the nuns received sentences of between five and eight years.

THE MYSTERY OF ELIZABETH KNAPP

Massachusetts was a bad place for demons in the 17th century. If reports are to be believed, there was a veritable plague of demonic possessions, of which the most famous resulted in the Salem witch trials. But Salem wasn't the only, or first, place to be afflicted.

Elizabeth Knapp, the daughter of a farmer, was 16 when she apparently became possessed by a demon in 1671. She was working as a servant in the household of the Puritan preacher Samuel Willard in Groton, 50km (31 miles) northwest of Boston, Massachusetts. Luckily for Knapp, Willard was more sympathetic than many preachers might have been under the circumstances. He took a keen and benign interest in the case, and worked hard to diagnose and cure her condition.

Knapp first showed puzzling symptoms on Monday, 30 October 1671. Sitting by the fireside, she suddenly complained of pains in various parts of her body, first her leg, then her breast, and then her neck, claiming that she was being strangled. The next day, she was in a strange mood, sometimes weeping and sometimes laughing, making strange gestures, and in the evening screamed on apparently seeing two figures in the cellar.

When someone went to the cellar with her, she suddenly turned her head and stared steadfastly at a seemingly empty space, saying, 'What cheer, old man?' Later the same evening, she was suddenly thrown into the middle of the room, where she had a vigorous fit.

She continued in violent fits all week, and those around struggled to prevent her throwing herself into the fire. According to Willard, 'she was violent in bodily motions, leapings, strainings and strange agitations scarce to be held in bound by the strength of three or four, violent also in roarings and screamings representing a dark resemblance of hellish torments'. On the Wednesday, two days after her first attack, she claimed that a neighbour, generally considered to be pious and of good character, had come to her down the chimney and caused her first attack. The woman was summoned, and even though Elizabeth's eyes were firmly closed (as they generally were during her periods of distress), the girl recognized her and responded violently to her presence. Afterwards, though, Elizabeth admitted that Satan had deceived her and the woman had done her no harm – though Satan might have copied her form to come down the chimney to her.

The following day, Elizabeth gave an extravagant confession before many witnesses of how the Devil had frequently harassed her, demanding that she give herself to him and sign a covenant (contract), in exchange for which he would give her wealth, an easy life and other things that she found appealing. He had, she said, shown her a book written in blood which others had signed, and had entreated her to sign it, too. He had appeared more and more frequently to her over the preceding weeks and months so that now he was around the house almost constantly.

Elizabeth also claimed that he encouraged her to harm people. On one occasion, he had told her to kill Willard with a billhook while he slept. Willard had even met Elizabeth on the stairs carrying something that she hid behind her back and would not reveal – she said that she was confounded by him not being asleep when the Devil said that he would be, and so he escaped the gruesome fate planned for him. The Devil urged her to murder her parents, neighbours, Willard's family – and especially his youngest child, who she was to throw into the fire or the oven. He lured her to the well so that she might throw herself into it and drown, but in her entranced state she could not negotiate the wall of the well.

Willard noted carefully the progress of her symptoms and his attempts to help her. There was a lot of backtracking and confusion. Elizabeth would claim one thing one day and deny it later. She blamed the Devil putting words into her mouth, forcing her to make this excuse or that. For a long time she denied that she had

The billhook is a farming tool used for cutting branches and harvesting vegetation. Elizabeth Knapp claimed the Devil had instructed her to use one to slaughter preacher Samuel Willard.

signed the Devil's covenant, saying that she always rejected his demands no matter what blandishments he offered her. But having said that she never responded to the Devil's demands or went willingly with him, in late November she confessed that she had twice travelled with him between the towns of Groton and Lancaster, when he appeared in the form of a black dog with eyes in its back. She said that he pestered her because she would not sign his covenant or take notice of him.

Slowly she owned up to more and more involvement with the Devil. On 4 December, she told neighbours that the Devil had beset her for five years and she had finally resolved to sign his covenant because he would not leave her alone. However, she had failed to do so because she did not have a knife with which to cut herself so that she would bleed; it had to be signed in blood. On another occasion, the Devil presented her with a knife, by her account, but Willard's father intervened and took the knife from her.

A few days later, she told Willard that she had in fact signed the covenant. While she had been working at his house, she had seen an old man approach, crossing a meadow, and knew him to be the Devil. This time, when he demanded she sign the covenant, she agreed. She cut her finger with a knife and the Devil dipped a stick into her blood. She could not write, though, and he had to guide her hand while she wrote her name. The deal was that she would serve him for a year and he would serve her for six years, making her a witch. He showed her a vision of Hell, saying that if she was unfaithful to him, she would have to go there and suffer.

Afterwards, Elizabeth reflected that this was not a very good deal, as six years is not long compared to the eternity she could expect to spend in Hell as a consequence of making a deal with the Devil. Seeing her disquiet, the Devil continued to pester her for more of her blood and to sign his book again. She claimed that he said since she had already signed, she might as well do it again as the deed was done and sealed. She answered, not unreasonably, that if that was the case, he had no need to have her sign it again.

But neither did she stick to this version of events. On 10 December, she told Willard that she had not in fact signed the Devil's book, that she was discontented with her life as she found her work burdensome and was never happy. She had been tempted to try witchcraft, and had proclaimed that if the Devil came to her she would give herself to him, but she had never actually done it.

Then on 17 December she had a type of fit that convinced Willard she was indeed possessed by the Devil. She began by extending her tongue from her mouth 'most frightfully to an extraordinary length and greatness', and then adopting grotesque postures and distortions of her body. She proceeded to berate people around her and, when Willard entered, said to him, 'Oh! You are a great rogue.' Elizabeth spoke with a deep voice that seemed to come from her throat, and she did not move her lips at all. Willard concluded it was Satan speaking through her, but the voice denied it, saying 'I am not Satan, I am a pretty black boy; this is my pretty girl.'

On 19 December, Elizabeth told Willard that the Devil had entered into her through her mouth on the second night after her first recorded attack, and had never left her. On 22 December, the voice returned to her but this time crowed like a cockerel rather than speaking. Elizabeth was able to intimate by signs that the Devil planned to carry her away that night.

On 11 January she changed her story again, saying she had never made a covenant with the Devil, that although he had power over her body he had no power over her soul, and that her fits were caused by 'discontent'. She acknowledged that she had felt tempted to murder people, and that it seemed as if someone with twice her power was trying to force her to do it. She said she did not know whether the Devil was in her and, if he was, she did not know when he had entered her. When she was taken with fits of speechlessness, she felt as if a string were tied around the root of her tongue and pulled it down within her when she tried to speak. Willard had noted that during these fits her tongue was curled at the top of her mouth and could not be moved even by inserting his fingers into her mouth.

Willard's narrative ends on 15 January, when Elizabeth had been silent and having fits for many days. He states his conclusions that she is not feigning her fits – she is too strong, sometimes needing several men to restrain her, for them to be faked. Further, the voice she uses is not her own and he believes it could be demonic. He says that he cannot decide whether she has made a pact with the Devil as her accounts are contradictory. He pleads that people show compassion towards her, and see in her 'a monument to divine severity' which might lead all who see her to 'fear and tremble'.

There is no record of what happened to Elizabeth, whether she recovered or continued to have fits until her death. She was not tried as a witch or for any other crime – there would be a record of that. We shall probably never know what became of her.

SPIRITS OF THE WAVE

On 11 March 2011, an earthquake off the coast of Tōhoku, Japan, caused a massive tsunami which swept ashore, destroying buildings and infrastructure up to 10km (6¼ miles) inland. Around 16,000 people died and another 2,500 were recorded as missing. For the Japanese, with their strong belief in ancestor spirits and the link between the living and the dead, those deaths represented a catastrophic influx of *gaki*, or 'hungry ghosts' – spirits of the dead who have been brutally severed from ties with the living by a sudden, unmourned death or by the destruction or neglect of their shrines.

There are many shades of belief, but the essential features are fairly consistent. A person who has died is treated still as a member of the family; their memory is venerated, with a *butsudan* (household altar) and and *ihai* (memorial tablet). They slip slowly into the past as long as all is handled well, with due respect and reverence. It was against this background of a deep link between the living and the dead that disaster struck northeast Japan. The tsunami destroyed entire families, leaving no one to mourn and venerate. It left the living numbed and confused, and without the resources to do what the dead needed. Often there was no body to bury.

Even families who did not lose any living members often lost the shrines to their ancestors; their destruction meant the dead ancestors lost their mooring in the world of the living. Some people even died in the disaster because they went back to their houses to collect their *ihai*, unwilling to leave their dead ancestors behind.

The survivors suffered as displaced spirits were released into their environment. Within days, people reported seeing ghosts. It was not just the distraught bereaved claiming to see their lost loved ones.

GHOSTS V. TOURISTS

After the Asian tsunami of 2004, the tourist industry in badly hit areas such as Thailand suffered greatly. A few years later, when resorts had been rebuilt, European, American and Australasian tourists returned to the region, but Asian tourists stayed away. Their belief that the ghosts of the unburied dead would still haunt the area made it an impossible choice for a holiday destination. Two years after the disaster, the prime minister of Thailand, Thaksin Shinawatra, pleaded with Asian travellers, 'Please tell your fellow Japanese and Chinese back home to stop fearing ghosts and return to this region again.'

People reported a dead neighbour coming to visit temporary homes in a refugee settlement, sitting in a chair for a while and leaving the seat wet with seawater. A fire station in Tagajo received calls to come to areas where all the buildings had been destroyed – there could be no fire, no further disaster. But when the fire crews drove to the ruins anyway and prayed for the spirits of the dead, the ghostly calls stopped. One taxi driver picked up a passenger who asked to go to an address that the driver knew had been destroyed. Part way there, the man disappeared from the back seat. The taxi driver continued to the ruined address, and opened the door for his invisible passenger. One man reported seeing the eyes of the dead staring from puddles when it rained. Tohoku University began to catalogue the stories relating to what one Buddhist priest wrote about as 'the ghost problem'.

Unfortunately, the spirits did not restrict themselves to taking taxis, making hoax calls or alarming neighbours. Some apparently took up residence in survivors, leading to a flurry of reports of possession by spirits of the tsunami dead.

Reverend Kaneda was chief priest at a Zen temple in Kurihara, nearly 50km (31 miles) inland from the coast where the tsunami struck, but still he had direct contact with relatives of the dead and even with those who seemed to be possessed by spirits of victims. He told the journalist Richard Lloyd Parry about two cases of apparent possession he had dealt with.

One was a man, a builder, who was personally untouched by the disaster and found it hard to accept its reality. He and his wife had driven to the coast to see the devastation for themselves, but it became a grim outing. He had put a sign on his car claiming it to be a disaster relief vehicle, so that he could get through unhindered. They returned home sobered by what they had seen.

That night, his family ate dinner normally, but he was far from normal afterwards. According to his wife – he had no memory of the events – he jumped down onto all fours and began snarling and licking the ground, squirming like a beast, and then saying, 'You must die. You must die. Everyone must die. Everything must die and be lost.'

He then ran to a field in front of the house and rolled over and over in the mud, just as though he were being tumbled around in the sea, shouting: 'There, over there! They're all over there – look!' Eventually his wife dragged him back to the house, where he continued to shout until the early morning. Then he complained that something was pressing on him and collapsed into sleep.

The next night he saw figures walking past the house: parents and children, an old man with a child, a group of friends, all covered in mud. He said that they stared at him, but he was not afraid, just puzzled by their muddy clothes. The following day he was tired, after fitful sleep, and staggered around the house snarling abuse at his wife. 'Drop dead!' he said to her, 'Everyone else is dead, so die!' His wife took him to the temple, where Kaneda beat a drum and recited the Heart Sutra over him. At the end, Kaneda splashed him with holy water and he regained his senses and a feeling of calm. His nose felt bunged up, and as he drove home, bright pink jelly poured from it.

After speaking to Kaneda he believed that his flippant visit to the devastated shore had angered the ghosts of those who had died so recently and traumatically. He had not approached the scene with due reverence. As a result he had been invaded by the spirits not just of human victims but even of some animal casualties of the tsunami – hence the time he spent snarling and rolling in the mud like a dog.

Kaneda also told the story of a 25-year-old nurse who had come to him. She had first telephoned, in great distress, saying she wanted to kill herself and that some kind of 'things' were entering her. Her mother and fiancé brought her to the temple. Her fiancé said she repeatedly complained of something pushing into her from a place 'below' and the presence of the dead pouring out all around her. Just as exorcists in the West have done for centuries, Kaneda spoke to whatever was possessing her, asking who it was and what it wanted.

The spirit spoke with an odd voice – not the woman's own voice – and went on for three hours. It turned out to be the spirit of a young woman who had killed herself. Her mother had remarried and she, feeling unwanted, had run away to work in the 'water trade', a dark world of clubs and prostitution. She fell victim to an unpleasant and manipulative man, and when she killed herself no one had mourned her death or lit incense sticks for her. Kaneda encouraged the spirit to come into the light, to leave the young woman, and he sprinkled holy water. He recited sutras for her. At last the nurse came to her senses, the spirit gone.

But it was not the last Kaneda saw of her. She returned three days later, having been possessed by another spirit. This time she complained of pain in her left leg, and when Kaneda encouraged her to stop struggling against the spirit and 'let it in', it spoke in the gruff voice of an old seaman. The spirit claimed to have been a naval officer, killed during the Second World War after being injured in the leg. Again Kaneda freed the nurse from the spirit's hold over her.

This went on for many months. All the spirits had some connection with water, though not all were connected with the tsunami. Among those that were was a middle-aged man who was calling out desperately for his daughter, Kaori. When the earthquake struck, he had driven to her school by the coast to save her, but had been drowned. When Kaneda asked where he was, the spirit replied that he was at the bottom of the sea, and that it was very cold. Another man had committed suicide after his two daughters were killed by the tsunami. And another, who had drowned, worried about his widow who was unhappy, living alone in a metal hut and keeping a rope in a shoebox which he feared she would use to hang herself.

Kaneda patiently helped each spirit to the light, sometimes more than one a night. As soon as the nurse returned to work, she felt the dead pressing around her again and was possessed after only a few days. On one occasion, she came to Kaneda saying that she was surrounded by dogs, and complaining loudly that she did not want to be possessed by a dog. At last she relented. Three men tried to hold her down while the dog spirit took over her body, but they could not control her. She roared and pawed at the ground while Kaneda read the sutras over her. When the dog spirit had left, she revealed that it was the ghost of a dog that had been killed at Fukishima. The nuclear reactor at the electricity power station there had been damaged by the earthquake and released radioactivity into the surrounding area, leading to evacuation. The dog had been left chained up and died of thirst and hunger. She revealed that people in hazard suits had peered into the kennel and seen the body of the dog.

Eventually, the woman learned to have some control and resistance. Although she still perceived the spirits, they could not harass and possess her against her will. But Kaneda was understandably relieved when she and her fiancé moved away from the area.

A woman offers flowers to the sea for the spirits of those who died in the tsunami. As of 2015, the death toll stood at approximately 16,000 deaths and more than 2,500 people missing. To this day, taxi drivers in some of the worst-affected areas tell stories of 'phantom fares' where spirits ask for rides to places that were destroyed by the huge waves, before disappearing.

THE LOUDUN POSSESSIONS

The most famous case of mass hysteria related to supposed supernatural activity is surely the Salem witch trials of the 1690s in America. But it was certainly not the first case. The phenomenon began in France, in Aix-en-Provence, in 1611 but became well known with the so-called Loudun possessions in 1632. In France, the charge was not one of witchcraft per se, but that certain priests had caused young nuns to be possessed by demons.

The unfortunate priest at the heart of the case was Urbain Grandier, an attractive and charismatic man who preferred simpler forms of faith and worship to the ornate rituals of the Catholic Church. His perceived Reformist leanings, and the Huguenots who made up part of his congregation, made him unpopular with the mainstream church. He was, though, apparently popular with the ladies. He is reported to have had lovers – not ideal in a priest, but neither was it particularly uncommon. In 1630, he was charged with immorality, but acquitted (probably with the help of friends in high places) and returned to his job as parish priest in Loudun. But when he hoped to gain the post of confessor to the Ursuline nuns of the convent at

Loudun, his reputation as a bit of a lothario went against him and the job went instead to Abbé Mignon.

There are two conflicting accounts of what happened next. One version is that the Bishop of Poitiers – who had previously, perhaps reluctantly, acquitted Grandier – approached Mignon with a plan to discredit Grandier by persuading the nuns to feign possession and blame him for it. The other version is that the nuns spontaneously approached Mignon with a request for exorcism. The principal source for the incident is a history written at the time (1634), which is very partial, painting Urbain Grandier in an extremely bad light. It is doubtful that we will ever know which version is true. But whether it was a ploy or not, it did not go well for Grandier over the ensuing months.

The prioress in charge of the convent, Jeanne des Anges, together with the sub-prioress, Sister de Colombiers, and a junior nun called Marthe de Saint-Monique, reported nightly appearances of an apparition of a man of the cloth asking for their help. Some accounts say that the nuns complained of sexual dreams (which they later said were about Grandier), that they cried out in the night, and that no amount of fasting and flagellation in the daytime brought them any relief from these night-time assaults.

After trying medical remedies to no avail, they had no option but to call on the assistance of the confessor,

Abbé Mignon. Making their trouble public was a trial to them. Not only was it embarrassing to admit to demonic possession, but both patrons and pupils distanced themselves from the convent, which would spell financial disaster.

Mignon attempted an exorcism, and was apparently most surprised and alarmed to discover the possessing spirit to denounce Grandier as the instigator of the evil affair. In all, seventeen nuns, including Jeanne des Anges, were 'found to be either fully possessed, or partially under the influence of the Evil One'. More serious attempts at exorcism were clearly called for.

The exorcisms were performed by expert exorcists: a Capuchin, Father Tranquille; a Franciscan, Father Lactance; and a Jesuit, Father Jean-Joseph Surin. They became public spectacles, taking place on a stage erected in the cathedral in front of 7,000 spectators, and with the nuns brought in chained. During exorcism, the nuns would commonly have violent convulsions that led to barking, shrieking, contortions, and lewd approaches to the exorcists. A contemporary account paints a vivid picture of the scenes:

'[The nuns] struck their chests and backs with their heads, as if they had their necks broken, and with inconceivable rapidity; they twisted their arms at the joints of the shoulder, the elbow, or the wrist, two or three times around. Lying on their stomachs, they joined the palms of their hands to the soles of their feet; their faces became so frightful one could not bear to look at them; their eyes remained open without winking. Their tongues issued suddenly from their mouths, horribly swollen, black, hard, and covered with pimples, and yet while in this state they spoke distinctly. They threw themselves back till their heads touched their feet, and walked in this position with wonderful rapidity, and for a long time. They uttered cries so horrible and so loud that nothing like it was ever heard before. They made use of expressions so indecent as to shame the most debauched of men, while their acts, both in exposing themselves and inviting lewd behaviour from those present, would have astonished the inmates of the lowest brothels in the country.'

The nuns used 'oaths and blasphemous expressions so execrable, so unheard of, that they could not have suggested themselves to the human mind'. They could, witnesses heard, stay awake and fast for five or six days at a stretch and endure the torments of possession twice a day for hours at a time without showing ill effects. Indeed, some even seemed healthier than before.

Bizarre behaviour characterized their exorcisms. They would fall asleep spontaneously, their bodies becoming so heavy that even a strong man could not move their heads. Strange voices could be heard quarrelling inside Françoise Filestreau, several speaking at the same time, as the demons argued about who should have control of her speech. She had her mouth closed the whole time. Elizabeth Blanchard would stand on her head in her convulsions, and Jeanne des Anges herself could be suspended in the air 60cm (2ft) above the ground, or on one occasion rested with only her elbow on the ground. The nuns could move from lying prone to standing upright without moving a muscle.

Their contortions were prodigious:

'Others, when comatose, became supple like a thin piece of lead, so that their body could be bent in every direction, forward, backward, or sideways, till their head touched the ground; and they remained thus so long as their position was not altered by others.

'At other times they passed the left foot over their shoulder to the cheek. They passed also their feet over their head till the big toe touched the tip of the nose.

'Others again were able to stretch their legs so far to the right and left that they sat on the ground without any space being visible between their bodies and the floor, their bodies erect and their hands joined.

'One, the Mother Superior, stretched her legs to such an extraordinary extent, that from toe to toe the distance was 7 feet, though she was herself but 4 feet high.'

Witnessed accounts of their behaviour were sent to the Sorbonne in Paris, where doctors confirmed that this was evidence of demonic possession.

Jeanne des Anges (or a demon speaking through her) claimed that the nuns were possessed by two demons called Asmodeus and Zabulon, saying that the possession had begun after Grandier (allegedly) left a bunch of musk roses in the convent. He had, she claimed, been visiting them (in spirit, not in person) in the convent for many months, inciting them to commit lewd acts.

The nuns were shown to be able to speak in languages they did not know, a well-known symptom of demonic possession. These included Spanish, Turkish, German and Italian. A certain M. de Launay de Razilli, who had lived in America, claimed to have questioned one of the nuns in a Native American language and received a cogent reply. When Grandier was allowed to challenge the demons in his defence, none was able to answer his questions in Greek. This did him little good, though, as one spirit/nun then explained that the demons had forbidden them to speak in Greek.

THE SHOW TRIAL

The exorcisms did not free the nuns from their evil spirits, and the night-time assaults continued unabated. Inevitably, the exorcisms led to the accusation and prosecution of Grandier. The trial was something of a political hot potato. The French court became involved, and Cardinal Richelieu decided to continue with proceedings against Grandier, even allowing the evidence of demons (those speaking through the nuns) against him. Louis XIII approved the move.

Richelieu had good reasons to want rid of the cleric. The cardinal was encouraging Louis XIII to remove power from the local towns and centralize it; the intellectual Grandier knew what was going on and opposed it. The authorities hoped that a quick trial and conviction would end the possessions. They were to be disappointed.

Urbain Grandier was arrested and his investigation began. As was customary, he was stripped naked and shaved of all head and body hair. He was then examined by a 'surgeon' who found three 'Devil's marks' on his body. A Devil's mark was usually characterized as a blemish which could be pricked with a needle and cause neither pain not bleeding. This was, of course, open to abuse. Many examiners had rounded telescopic probes which collapsed under pressure on the skin, so causing no immediate harm to the accused – though infinite later harm in that it identified them as a witch. According to Nicholas Aubin, writing in 1693, this was used in the search for marks on Grandier's body; the objections of a surgeon and apothecary were rejected. One piece of evidence held weight at the time, but might now be said to weaken the case against him and support the suspicion that he was stitched up. This was a signed contract with the Devil, supposedly in Grandier's hand, and to which not just Grandier himself but also Beelzebub and some other demons had put their signatures.

At one point, some of the possessed seem to have had a change of heart and tried to retract their statements. Jeanne des Anges even turned up with a noose around her neck saying that she would hang herself if she could not withdraw her earlier lies. But a powerful nobleman, Laubardemont (who, it turns out, was related to Jeanne), stated that anyone who testified in favour of Grandier would have their belongings seized and be declared a traitor. That put a stop to the defence. Finally, seventy-two witnesses gave evidence against him.

The court tortured Grandier relentlessly, using in particular the 'boot', a structure that constrained the leg and into which wooden wedges were driven with a hammer, putting unbearable pressure on the leg. He did not confess, recant or denounce anyone, despite both legs being broken by this horrendous torture. It was reported that he refused Holy Water and would not call on God, Christ or the Holy Virgin in his torment. Aldous Huxley observed, not unreasonably, that since all this was being done in the name of religion it's not altogether surprising that he did not appeal to that same religion in the midst of his sufferings. In a distorted logic, his accusers noted that his refusal to admit to his sorcery under torture was further evidence of his guilt, as such pacts with the Devil inevitably include a clause requiring the witch to deny their involvement. The Devil apparently hardens the victim's heart to make them able to bear the torture without reneging on this promise.

Despite his lack of confession, Urbain Grandier was found guilty and sentenced to be burned at the stake. Although it was customary for victims to be strangled before burning, as the executioner stepped forward with the rope the flames leapt up and set fire to it, so Grandier was denied this final reprieve from agony and was plunged still living into the flames. Apparently, a flock of pigeons or doves flew around and around the stake, and could not be driven away even by archers. While Grandier's Huguenot supporters claimed this was evidence of the Holy Ghost showing his innocence, the accusers said the birds were demons.

Yet still the possessions continued, and so did the exorcisms. They became something of a tourist attraction, with spectators keen to see nuns cavorting around, walking on their hands, lifting up their skirts and acting lewdly. Grandier was executed in 1634, and

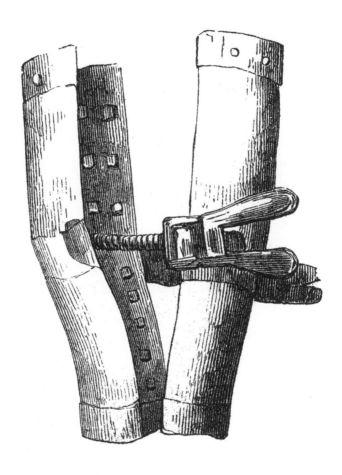

The boot was a Medieval torture device designed to cause crushing injuries to the foot or leg and was used to interrogate Urbain Grandier.

the exorcisms continued until 1637, when Jeanne was finally declared free of the demons that had possessed her.

> 'Each day they were exorcised in the various churches of the town. Jeanne des Anges attracted particular attention by the violence of her fits, the obscenity of her language, and her cynical postures . . . The inventions of the most licentious imagination would find it difficult to come anywhere near the facts. The pen refuses to set down here the cynical actions which were customary with Jeanne des Anges and her companions, and the obscene remarks to which they incessantly gave utterance.'

Abbé Lactance, who assisted the possessed women, was himself said to fall victim to possession some time later. First the carriage he was riding in turned over unaccountably on a smooth road, and then he 'experienced the greatest vexations from the demons, who at times deprived him of sight, and at times of memory; they produced in him violent fits of nausea, dulled his intelligence, and worried him in numerous ways'. Father Tranquille, the exorcist, suffered a fate that was said to be the same, but sounds rather different in all regards except the putative cause, demons: 'They cast him to the ground, they cursed and swore out of his mouth, they caused him to put out his tongue and hiss like a serpent, they filled his mind with darkness, seemed to crush out his heart, and overwhelmed him with a thousand other torments.' The surgeon who had found the Devil's marks on Grandier saw visions of him before he died. For days, he lay shaking and apparently mad in his bed, speaking to Grandier, who he believed was in front of him. Grandier's supporters saw this as the result of guilt at what he had knowingly done.

Jeanne des Anges was the lucky one. Under continued exorcisms by Abbé Surin, she was freed from the demons and became possessed instead by benevolent spirits. In her final session, he demanded that the possessing spirit leave her and write the name of the Virgin on her arm. She held up her arm to show the name 'Maria' written clearly on her hand. Her release was celebrated with a *Te Deum*.

But Surin was not so lucky. He, too, became haunted by the exorcisms in the end – he had, indeed, offered his own spirit in atonement for the sacrilege he witnessed at Loudun. As Jeanne got better, his condition worsened. Over a period of twenty years, he was periodically unable to eat, dress himself, walk, read, write, or pray, and tried unsuccessfully to kill himself by jumping out of a window. When it was time to preach, though, contemporaries reported he was divinely inspired and his words soared, even though he had been unable to do any preparation. He recovered eight years before his death in 1665.

Father Urbain Grandier was accused of summoning demons in 1634.

SETTING THE PARAMETERS OF POSSESSION

Although the Loudun possessions became the largest and most famous case in 17th-century France, the first two decades of the century saw a great increase in charges of witchcraft and possession. One of the most important was at Aix-en-Provence in 1611, as this changed the legal standing of the victim of possession. Before this, the testimony of a possessed person was not admitted in court since – quite reasonably – while in the throes of possession it was actually the demon's testimony rather than the individual's, and demons are arch-liars who cannot be trusted an inch. The testimony of the demoniac was allowed at Aix; this set the precedent for the testimony of Jeanne des Anges which would condemn Urbain Grandier in Loudun twenty years later.

The first signs of trouble appeared in Madeleine de Demandolx de la Palud, a 17-year-old Ursuline nun with a history of mental instability. She was frequently sent home from the convent to her parents when she suffered bouts of depression. Sister Catherine de Gaumer, head of the convent at Marseilles, heard that Madeleine was having an affair with a priest, Father

Louis Gaufridi. She told Madeleine's mother, and instructed Father Gaufridi he must not contact the girl. When Madeleine gave a full account of her relationship with Gaufridi, Sister Catherine had her moved to the convent at Aix to prevent any further trouble. But two years later, Madeleine showed signs of demonic possession, destroying a crucifix and contorting her body in bizarre and unnatural ways.

Attempts at exorcism failed to cure her, but they did open a whole new can of worms. Madeleine denounced Father Gaufridi as a devil-worshipper who had been having sex with her for two years. More cases of possession were uncovered, and by the end of 1609 a total of eight nuns at Aix were considered possessed. The worst case was deemed to be that of Louise Capeau, who was tormented with the most extreme contortions.

The Grand Inquisitor Sebastien Michaelis and a Flemish exorcist, Father Domptius, were called to the convent at Aix; they found 666 demons to be infesting Madeleine. Father Gaufridi was called to exorcise Louise, but was then denounced as a sorcerer and cannibal. Louise accused him of all kinds of sexual perversion, which she claimed he had practised against her – like the later Loudun case, the possessions of Aix were highly sexualized. A search of Father Gaufridi's rooms for books of sorcery found no evidence to support the girls' claims.

When released from prison into his parish in Marseilles, Gaufridi demanded that his name be cleared. But appearing in court wasn't the good idea it had first seemed. Madeleine in particular, but also Louise, swung wildly between hurling bizarre accusations of all types of depravity at Gaufridi and retracting the claims. Madeleine was not beyond suspicion herself. She was searched for marks of the Devil, which were found, and she twice tried to kill herself as a consequence. Her explanation, though, was that Gaufridi had initiated her and the fact of her possession was his fault. The court, for the first time ever, accepted the evidence of a person deemed to be possessed – so they effectively admitting the testimony of a demon. It was a dire turning point.

Things were never going to go well for Father Gaufridi: having affairs with young nuns was not a good career move. But his fall from grace was extreme and horrendous. He was shaved and searched for the Devil's mark, and three marks were found. This was enough to damn him. He was tortured using strappado, in which the victim is suspended by the arms, tied behind his back, dislocating the shoulders. At his court hearing, a confession extracted under torture was supported by a document purporting to be a covenant with the Devil written in his own blood. He tried to retract the confession, which included the claim that

Father Gaufridi was tortured using strappado, also known as corda, where his hands were tied behind his back and he was suspended by a rope attached to the wrists. Added weights intensified the pain. This technique typically resulted in dislocated shoulders.

he had staged a Black Mass with the intention of gaining power over women, but the court did not allow it.

Inevitably, Father Gaufridi was condemned to death. He was dragged around the city for five hours before arriving at the stake where he was, mercifully, strangled before burning. Madeleine, who had renounced all the saints and every prayer ever said for her in front of the church, was reported to be immediately released from her possession as Gaufridi died. Louise was not so lucky; she remained possessed for the rest of her life.

Both girls were banished from the convent, and Madeleine was twice charged with witchcraft. On the second occasion, the Devil's marks were found on her again and she was imprisoned, but released into the custody of a relative. Despite her troubles, she lived to the age of seventy-seven.

HYSTERIA BREAKS OUT AGAIN . . .

There were many other cases of mass hysteria/ possession in French convents over the course of the 17th century, but not all led to public trials. Ten years after Loudun, quite a remarkable case occurred at Louviers – remarkable because of the number of supposedly possessed people involved, but also on account of the extraordinary sexual content of the case, recorded in detail. When cases are recorded by priests, they sometimes gloss over the more salacious details as 'too offensive to record'. There was no such squeamishness in this case. This time, eighteen nuns became possessed, beginning again with a very young girl, 18-year-old Sister Madeleine Bavent. During the course of the exorcisms and trial, though, the hysteria spread beyond the convent and began to engulf the entire town of Louviers.

Madeleine first accused the director of the convent, Mathurin Picard, and the vicar at Louviers, Father Thomas Boulle, of abducting her and taking her and other nuns to a witches' sabbat where she had to marry the Devil, named Dagon, and perform sexual acts with him on the altar. Two other men, she said, were crucified and disembowelled while this was going on.

Other nuns made similar claims, including having sex with demons, especially Dagon. One nun, Sister Barbara of St Michael, was said to be possessed by the demon Ancitif. The nuns claimed, too, that the Devil, in the form of Picard and Boulle, tried to lead them into heresy through complex theological arguments against established doctrine.

Madeleine Bavent's earlier life was not easy. Orphaned at a young age, she was brought up by an aunt in Rouen. At the age of thirteen she began work sewing church vestments and at eighteen was seduced (or perhaps raped) by a Franciscan, Father Bontemps, who came to inspect the work of the seamstresses. Madeleine left to join the Franciscans as a nun in Louviers.

The first chaplain of the convent was Father Pierre David, who was sympathetic to the heresy of the Illuminati. Among the beliefs of the Illuminati were that Christians should worship God naked, following the example of Adam, and that any kind of act was acceptable as long as the person had devout intent and inner calm. As a consequence, the nuns were accustomed to receive holy communion naked and fast for eight to ten days. This was supposed to be a sign of their humility and poverty, but it's difficult not to think it looks a bit suspect.

Madeleine spent three years as a novice under this guidance, and took communion with her breasts exposed. In her later account – and we don't know how reliable that was – she reported that Father David encouraged the nuns to go around naked a lot of the time, taking this as a sign of being holy and virtuous. She said also that he encouraged them to fondle each other and commit 'foul and sinful' acts. One of the stunts involved a mock circumcision of a giant phallus which some of the nuns then used for sexual gratification. Father David apparently never had sex with Madeleine, though they indulged in 'indecent caresses'. When Father David died, Father Mathurin Picard, assisted by Father Thomas Boullé, took over. Madeleine said that they continued the indecent practices, and though she never went naked (as the other nuns accused her of doing) she was often fondled by Father Boullé and he sometimes raped her, resulting in a pregnancy. Nothing is known of any pregnancy or baby she might actually have had.

This much might be all too plausible, but some of Madeleine's claims are more outlandish. She reported that Father Picard made love philtres that drove some of the nuns to do 'most filthy acts' with him, and that these were made from sacramental wafers sopped with clots of menstrual blood (which suggests at least some degree of co-operation on the part of the nuns). He then buried these in the convent gardens. Other philtres were more gruesome, including entrails from slain babies, broken limbs from dead bodies and 'blood which trickled from the holy wafer'.

Madeleine continued to claim that she attended a sabbat once or twice a week, falling into a trance or ecstasy at around 11 pm. At the sabbat were Fathers Picard and Boullé, three or four nuns from the convent, some lay people from the town and some half-human, half-bestial demons. The priests said a Black Mass which was a parody of the real mass. This was followed by a feast, sometimes including roasted human flesh, and then the nuns copulated with the spirit of Father David or with one of the living priests, or a demon. Most bizarrely, she described the priests taking a large communion wafer, cutting a hole in the centre large enough to fit over a penis, and then copulating with the nuns with the wafer in situ. Madeleine also claimed to have been visited and raped by the Devil in the form of a black cat over a period of several years.

The bizarre orgies were said to have occurred between 1628 and 1642, when Father Picard died. Before his death, no one had said a word and no one suspected anything was amiss. It was only then that the nuns began to exhibit signs of possession. Father Esprit de Bosroger wrote that for four years they 'suffered the most frightful convulsions night and day . . . [with] paroxysms of constantly recurring frenzy, contortions, animal howlings, clamours and outcries'.

As had happened at Loudun, the exorcisms were held in public and became a popular spectacle. Father Boullé was being tortured at the same time, his screams adding an extra frisson of horror to the events. (As Mathurin Picard had already died he was spared this fate.) The nuns displayed the familiar signs of possession, including screaming and achieving superhuman contortions and strength. One nun was reported to have 'ran with movements so abrupt that it was difficult to stop her. One of the clerics present, having caught her by the arm, was surprised to find that it did not prevent the rest of her body from turning over and over as if the arm were fixed to the shoulder merely by a spring'.

A physician, Dr Yvelin, doubted the veracity of the possessions and said that he saw signs of deceit, but on the whole they were accepted as genuine. The other nuns confessed to whatever they were accused of and promptly blamed Madeleine in order to save themselves.

Almost everyone who attended the exorcisms was interrogated by the inquisitors and the hysterical symptoms of possession spread through the whole town. The outcome was unhappy: Madeleine was imprisoned in an underground dungeon, fed only bread and water three days a week. She was cruelly mistreated, and tried to kill herself on several occasions, but finally died in her prison in 1647.

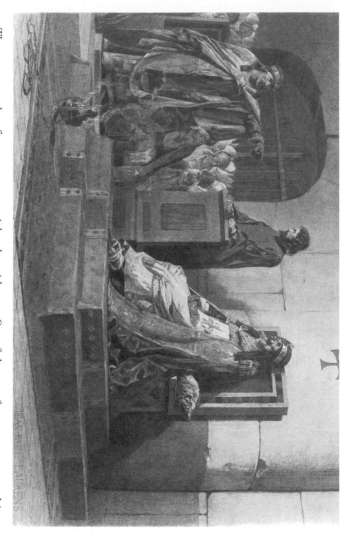

There was precedent for post-mortem trial and punishment. One of the most famous cases occurred in 897 AD, when the body of Pope Formosus was exhumed nine months after his death and put on trial in the so-called Cadaver Synod. He was found guilty of breaching church law. Two of his fingers were cut off and his body was thrown into the River Tiber.

Mathurin Picard did not entirely escape justice: his corpse was exhumed, excommunicated, and thrown on a rubbish heap. When his family found it, they demanded an investigation, which was carried out by the Parlement at Rouen. The case dragged on for four years. In the end, the exumation was condemned, but Father Picard was found guilty of witchcraft and his corpse was burned, presumably on the grounds that punishment came better late than never.

Father Boullé was the most unfortunate. He was convicted, tortured so that he might reveal his accomplices (odd, as his accomplice was already dead) and then 'his head and feet being bare, clad only in his shirt, having a cord about his neck, and holding in his hand a lighted taper of two pounds weight' was drawn on a hurdle to the market square on 21 August 1647 and there burned alive, his ashes being scattered to the four winds

SIGNS OF POSSESSION

As a result of the Louviers possession, the authorities came up with a guide to identifying possession which could be used in investigating future cases.

The agreed signs of possession were:

1 To think oneself possessed.

2 To lead a wicked life.

3 To live outside the rules of society.

4 To be persistently ill, falling into heavy sleep and vomiting unusual objects (either such natural objects as toads, serpents, maggots, iron, stones, and so forth; or such artificial objects as nails or pins).

5 To utter obscenities and blasphemies.

6 To be troubled with spirits ('an absolute and inner possession and residence in the body of the person').

7 To show a frightening and horrible countenance.

8 To be tired of living.

9 To be uncontrollable and violent.

10 To make sounds and movements like an animal.

11 To deny knowledge of fits after the paroxysm has ended.

12 To show fear of sacred relics and sacraments.

13 To curse violently at any prayer.

14 To exhibit acts of lewd exposure or abnormal strength.

'JESUS IS VICTOR!'

Gottliebin Dittus was a young German girl, living in Möttlingen in Württemberg, southern Germany, when she fell victim to signs of demonic possession in 1840. The first assault seems to have come while she was praying. The young girl fell unconscious to the floor, and after that was afflicted by hallucinations and poltergeist activity. She reported seeing shapes and lights at night-time, and her arms were smacked violently together against her will; she frothed at the mouth and suffered unexplained bleeding. She lost several jobs on account of her problems. Unexplained noises came from the house, too, which were so loud that people in the neighbourhood could hear them.

The local pastor, Reverend Blumhardt, visited her occasionally but was repelled by her behaviour. A woman from the village and Gottliebin's own doctor stayed overnight at her house and confirmed that the noises, at least, were real. Two years after her first attack, Gottliebin's brothers and sisters called on Reverend Blumhardt for help. Eventually, he and seven companions visited her in the house. As he entered the house, two loud noises, like gunshots, rang out. During the time the men were in the house they heard a total of twenty-five such sounds, some so loud that the windows rattled, plaster fell from the ceiling and chairs jumped on the floor. The men could find nothing in the house that would cause the noises, despite an exhaustive search.

Reverend Blumhardt visited repeatedly after that. Over the following two months, he explored Gottliebin's past and discovered that as a child she had been abused by her guardian, an aunt, who had exposed her to the practices of a popular peasant religion common in the area. He determined this to be the cause of her problems, and that she was possessed by demons. With no other way of dealing with the situation, he set about following the pattern he saw set by Christ in the Bible and embarked on a programme of fasting and praying for Gottliebin.

He and Gottliebin prayed together daily for the next two years in sessions which often became battles with her demons. Although her problems quietened when Gottliebin herself prayed, nothing gave her lasting respite.

Gottliebin was often hostile towards the reverend, clenching her fists, moving as though to scratch out his eyes, and swearing at him. She would hit the men who came with Reverend Blumhardt, but did not physically assault him personally. He responded with prayers, which seemed to banish the demons for a while, allowing Gottliebin to be herself for a short time. After a while, Reverend Blumhardt discovered that the demons would leave if he commanded them to do so.

The demons left a few at a time, first three, then seven, with Gottliebin's condition becoming worse and worse all the time. At one point, she complained of a fiery hand gripping her throat, trying to strangle her. When she said it had released her, her throat was covered with blisters. Reverend Blumhardt found the process exhausting, yet the demons kept coming, each announcing itself in its own voice. As the demons made themselves known, Gottliebin's face and voice changed, she beat her head against the wall, pulled her hair and hit out at those around her. For a while, she seemed improved and could live normally for a few weeks, but then the attacks returned with at least as much vigour as before. On one occasion, Gottliebin seemed to run mad, calling for a knife with which to kill herself, then climbing onto a window ledge ready to throw herself out. A flash of lightning brought her to herself and she came down from the window, but a new fit followed and she fetched a rope with which to hang herself. Again a flash of lightning brought her to her senses.

In February 1843, her condition changed once more for the worse. She began to vomit, but brought up first sand and then objects, including shards of glass, old, bent nails, pins and needles. Some came from her nose and ears as well as her mouth, and all were accompanied by terrible pain. Later she vomited locusts, a frog, bats and even a snake.

At Christmas of that year, her brother and sister began to have the same type of attack. Speaking through her sister, Katharina, one demon challenged God to show a sign that the whole of Möttlingen could witness.

A demonic voice again spoke through Gottliebin, saying, 'Now the game is up. Everything has been betrayed. You have ruined us completely. Alas, alas, everything is lost! We are 1,067, but there are many others still alive, and they ought to be warned! Oh woe [to] them, they are lost . . . Nobody could have driven us out! Only you managed it, you with your persistent praying!' After crying out in despair and shaking, Katharina suddenly bent her head and body far backwards and screamed out '*Jesus ist Sieger*!' (Jesus is Victor!)

This marked the end of the sisters' possession. Over a period of two years, a thousand demons had been expelled. Gottliebin not only recovered from all the symptoms of her possession, but her previous lameness also healed. Having had one foot smaller than the other, her small foot now grew to normal size; earlier stomach problems disappeared, and a raised shoulder straightened. She went to live as a servant in the pastor's house and helped with his work, dealing with the many visitors who flocked to visit Möttlingen as the scene of a miraculous healing. He left the organized reformed church when forbidden to use a prayer as a means of healing the sick – the church had come under pressure from doctors, who considered Blumhardt to be infringing on their professional territory. He moved into an old, empty resort hotel in the nearby town of Bad Boll, where he continued to practise his healing ministry.

THE HELL-HOUSE OF LATOYA AMMONS

Tales of demonic possession aren't restricted to the past. One case as recent as 2012 captured the public imagination and – perhaps inevitably – led to a film 'based on a true story'. The claimed persecution of Latoya Ammons and her children by demons resembles many accounts of poltergeist activity, but is raised to the state of possession by the conviction of many of those involved. We see in Latoya's case a direct clash between two interpretations of the 'possessed' behaviour: the paranormal and the psychological.

Latoya moved into a house in Gary, Indiana, in November 2011 with her mother Rosa and her three children, boys aged seven and nine, and a twelve-year-old girl (their names have never been released). Almost immediately, she was bothered by swarms of black flies that filled the porch, even though it was midwinter. No matter how many she killed, more came. But far worse was to come.

> **WHAT DOES A HELL-HOUSE LOOK LIKE?**
> Latoya's single-storey house still stands in Carolina Street, Gary. It is constructed of white wood and has a large, enclosed porch on the front.

> There are three bedrooms, a living room, a bathroom and an open-plan kitchen. A door from the kitchen opens onto stairs to a basement. The main rooms have hardwood floors and the basement has a concrete floor.
>
> The American paranormal investigation celebrity Zak Bagans bought the Ammons house for $35,000 for his TV show *Ghost Adventurers*.

The family heard heavy footsteps on the stairs up from the basement late at night, and then the door between the stairs and the kitchen creaking open – but no one was there. The sounds continued even after they began locking the door at night. On one occasion, Rosa woke to see a man pacing the floor of the living room. She later found wet bootprints on the boards.

More bizarre happenings followed. One night, the women were awake at 2am, mourning a relative who had died. Latoya was in the room of her 12-year-old daughter and suddenly cried out to her mother. When Rosa went into the room, she saw the girl levitating – floating mid-air above her bed, still fast asleep. The women and other mourners surrounded the bed and prayed until at last the girl descended. When she woke up, she had no recollection of what had happened. The others present left the house and refused ever to return. As time passed, the children became exceptionally violent towards one another, especially in the presence of their mother but also in public.

Feeling that this was more than they could deal with alone, the two women sought help from local churches. Most refused to have anything to do with it, but officials at one suggested the house was plagued by evil spirits. They advised cleansing it by washing the rooms with bleach and ammonia and drawing crosses in oil on all the doors and windows. Latoya poured olive oil on her children's hands and feet, too, and drew crosses on their foreheads with the oil.

Two clairvoyants advised Latoya that the house was possessed by at least 200 demons and suggested that she move. But Latoya's family didn't have the money to move house. Instead, they followed the advice of another clairvoyant to construct an altar in the basement. They covered an end table with a white sheet and placed a candle on it, along with statues of the Holy Family (Mary, Joseph and Jesus). Dressed in white T-shirts, and with white scarves wrapped around their heads, Latoya and a companion began another cleansing ritual. They lit fires of sage and sulphur, starting at the top of the house and working their way down until every room was filled with smoke. Then Latoya drew a cross with the smoke and they walked from room to room while her companion read Psalm 91 from the Bible:

'You will not fear the terror of night,
nor the arrow that flies by day,
nor the pestilence that stalks in the darkness,
nor the plague that destroys at midday.'

For three days, there were no further odd occurrences. Then it all got worse. Some nights, it was so bad that the family moved into a hotel for the hours of darkness. Latoya and her children began to show symptoms which the family took to be signs of possession, though Rosa claimed she was not affected because she had been born with special protection from evil. The children's eyes bulged, they spoke in deeper voices than usual, and 'evil' smiles crossed their faces. The youngest spent time hiding in a closet talking to a boy no one else could see, who apparently talked about what it felt like to be killed.

Poltergeist-like activity became more pronounced. The seven-year-old flew out of the bathroom as if he had been thrown, and a headboard crashed into Latoya's daughter so hard she needed stitches for the wound it left. The girl reported to mental health workers that she sometimes felt as though something was holding her down and choking her, making it impossible to move or speak. A voice told her she would die in the next 20 minutes and never see her family again.

In April 2012, Latoya called in the family doctor, Dr Geoffrey Onyeukwu. He reported that he found visiting the house alarming, but noted that the family was delusional and experiencing hallucinations. His visit apparently produced a severe reaction in the children – or in the demons. The two boys cursed the doctor in 'demonic voices' and the youngest was 'lifted and thrown into the wall with nobody touching him', according to a report written by a child-services professional. The boys passed out and could not be brought back to consciousness, so one of the medical attendants called 911. Several ambulances and police officers attended and the boys were taken to the Methodist Hospital in Gary. The staff were not enthusiastic when Latoya said she wanted the children to be anointed with oil, and laughed at her. Although one child woke and behaved normally, the other screamed and thrashed so vigorously that it took five men to hold him down.

A children's services professional was appointed to investigate the family. They were looking for evidence of child abuse, or signs that Latoya was exploiting the children for attention, persuading them to act abnormally to support her story. The case worker appointed was Valerie Washington. When she first interviewed the family, the youngest boy bared his teeth and growled at her. He rolled his eyes back and grabbed his older brother's throat. His growling continued while Latoya spoke about the possession and her attempts to end it through religious means.

In a later interview, the younger boy stared at his brother and growled, then spoke in an 'unnatural' voice, saying, 'It's time to die – I will kill you.' The older boy, meanwhile, head-butted his grandmother in the stomach. She grabbed his hands and began to pray. This is the point at which one of the medical workers began to believe the boy might actually be possessed. His face took on a weird grin, and he 'glided' backwards up the wall, flipped over Rosa and landed on his feet. He didn't let go of her hands throughout.

The intake officer's report states that the nine-year-old complained that ghosts were attacking him and his brother, then 'became aggressive and walked up the wall as if he was walking on the floor and did a flip over the grandmother. The episode was witnessed by the psych counselor and DCS [Department of Child Services] worker FCM Washington.'

Although the report sounds calm, Washington and one other member of staff fled the room in fear. The boy could not repeat the feat when asked to by a medic, but had at that point returned to normal behaviour.

The next day was the younger boy's eighth birthday. After they celebrated briefly in the hospital, officials told Latoya that the children were not going home with her, but would be taken into care for the duration of the investigation at least. They cited emotional and spiritual distress as the reason for emergency action.

Psychologists described Latoya's interpretation of the phenomenon as 'delusional' and tried to encourage her to interpret her children's 'possession' in different ways, but without success. But other professionals involved in the case were more inclined to accept Latoya's interpretation of events.

The next step was an extreme one for a 21st-century hospital, police force and children's protection services to take. The hospital chaplain called Reverend Michael Maginot to ask him to exorcise the nine-year-old boy. Reverend Maginot first wanted to rule out medical causes for the children's condition and went to visit the house. After two hours, a bathroom light began to flicker on and off, but stopped each time he walked over to investigate. He put it down to demonic activity. Later, venetian blinds in the kitchen began to swing although there was no wind, and wet footprints appeared on the living room floor. Latoya complained of a headache, and Maginot placed a crucifix against her head. She immediately convulsed. He spent four hours in the house and was convinced by the time that he left that it was haunted by ghosts and the family was indeed being plagued by demons. He sprinkled holy water in every room and blessed the house with prayers and readings from the Bible before leaving. He advised Latoya and her mother to move out as he didn't consider it safe. They went to stay with relatives.

A week later, Rosa was back to escort the DCS family case manager and police officers as they examined the house. Latoya refused to go inside. The police reported various malfunctions of equipment during and after the visit, and one photo taken of the house seemed to show a blurred white figure and a smaller green figure when enlarged. Another officer took photos with an iPhone and said there seemed to be silhouettes of figures in some of them.

> 'We know that there's evil in that house, and we know that evil is ever-present. Why go where evil possibly is there? You have no idea what you may run into.'
>
> Captain Charles Austin, Gary police

The police began to believe in some kind of evil presence, though the mental health workers remained sceptical. Clinical psychologist Stacy Wright examined the youngest boy and reported that he acted possessed when challenged or when asked questions he didn't want to answer. After a while, his version of accounts became 'bizarre, fragmented and illogical', changing every time he told it. She concluded that he did not have a mental illness but had been co-opted by his mother to enter into her delusions about demons. The psychologist examining the other children came to the same conclusion.

> 'This appears to be an unfortunate and sad case of a child who has been induced into a delusional system perpetuated by his mother and potentially reinforced [by other relatives].'
>
> Stacy Wright, clinical psychologist

Child services workers required Latoya to stop talking to her children about demons and possession and encourage them to take responsibility for their own behaviour, not blame it on demons. The family was also to take part in therapy. Latoya was told to find a job and move out of the house plagued by 'paranormal activity'.

While Latoya worked on meeting those objectives, police and DCS officials continued to investigate strange happenings in the house. Reverend Maginot, a DCS family case officer named Samantha Ilic and the police visited the house again with Latoya and Rosa. Maginot suggested that if a murder had taken place in the house, that would explain the paranormal activity. The police dug up the dirt under an area of broken concrete at the foot of the basement stairs, but found nothing suspicious, and certainly no body or other evidence of murder. A police dog showed no interest in any part of the house. But not everyone was reassured. Samantha Ilic touched some slippery, sticky liquid in the basement and soon after her little finger began to feel odd and turn white. She felt a panic attack coming on and left the house, standing outside for the rest of the visit. Latoya soon complained of a headache and shoulder pain and also left the building.

A police officer noticed an oily substance dripping from blinds in one room. They cleaned it up, secured the room for 25 minutes and then looked again, to find it had returned. Reverend Maginot said it was a manifestation of a paranormal or demonic presence – which seems to be jumping to conclusions, since he had encouraged Latoya to smear the doors and windows with oil.

Maginot sought permission from his bishop, Dale Melczek, to perform an exorcism but was told to find a priest who had done it before. He asked around; other priests suggested he look for a short-form exorcism format on the internet. He performed a service of blessing on the house to expel evil spirits and a minor (two-hour) exorcism on Latoya, consisting of prayers, statements and an appeal to demons to leave her. Two police officers and Samantha Ilic, the DCS case officer, were present. Ilic said that it felt odd and as though someone were in the room, breathing down her neck. She had a series of medical problems and accidents over the coming month, which she linked to the case. In all she had three accidents involving broken bones and one of serious burns. Some of her friends avoided her because they thought something evil had attached itself to her. Only the least sceptical person would be convinced that her accidents had a paranormal cause, however, since one resulted from jet-skiing and another from running in flip-flops – both high-risk activities.

Maginot told Latoya to look up the names of the demons that had been plaguing her, and when she did so her computer kept shutting down spontaneously. Even so, she managed to identify Beelzebub, the lord of the flies, and some demons associated with tormenting children.

The bishop finally gave Maginot permission to perform a more powerful exorcism, backed by the Church. He carried out three rituals at his church in June 2012, two in English and one in Latin. Each time, he praised God and condemned the devil. He spoke more loudly as Latoya convulsed while – she said – the demons struggled to remain within her, inflicting pain and trying to hold on at the same time. She claimed the pain was as intense as childbirth. Each session ended with Latoya falling asleep, which Maginot interpreted as the demons trying to reduce the effect of the ritual. After three exorcisms, and moving to a house in Indianapolis which had been pre-blessed to prevent any demonic infestation starting up, Latoya was free of her demons. Her children were returned to her and neither the family nor the house has suffered any subsequent paranormal problems.

Latoya's experience is particularly interesting in that it brings together two different cultures in modern America. The superstitious police and DCS workers in Indiana were in direct conflict with the psychologists who represented the rationalist, scientific approach. Dealing with exactly the same accounts, they adopted two widely different frames of explanation. Unfortunately, the case is marred by sloppiness. The police relied on unofficial photographs, some taken with an iPhone. Many minor incidents – such as a malfunctioning radio and a fault in a police car – were linked with the possession, which reduced the credibility of those promoting it as a paranormal phenomenon. The exorcism focused on Latoya, although it was the children who were said to be showing signs of possession. In the end, we don't have to accept every reported case of demonic possession as an actual example, even if we want to give credence to the phenomenon of possession itself. Latoya's is one of the more dubious cases.

Beezlebub as 'lord of the flies'.

'A CONTEMPORARY AND CLEAR-CUT CASE OF DEMONIC POSSESSION'

Not all modern cases of alleged possession are as easily dismissed as that of Latoya Ammons. The case of 'Julia' was reported by Richard Gallagher, who is a board-certified psychiatrist in private practice and Associate Professor of Clinical Psychiatry at New York Medical College – not the sort of person we would expect to be readily hoodwinked or persuaded that it takes a demon to break your ankle if you run in flip-flops. Of course, people in all walks of life entertain all kinds of belief. Gallagher seems from his writings to be a committed Christian, and one who believes in the veracity of miracles. He is also clearly conversant with modern psychological diagnoses and so might be able to negotiate a path between the two cultures which, in Latoya Ammons's case, collided head-on.

'Julia' (not her real name) is a middle-aged white woman born in the USA and still resident there. She was brought up a Catholic, but had left the faith long before she sought help in the form of a Catholic exorcism. She had, in fact, been involved for many years with various Satanist groups. The team of professionals who investigated and assisted in Julia's case included, besides Gallagher, other qualified mental health personnel, at least four Catholic priests, a deacon and his wife, and two nuns (both of whom were trained nurses, and one a psychiatric nurse). Julia self-referred for treatment in 2008.

Gallagher noted that Julia exhibited many of the features common in people considered to be victims of demonic possession, including great strength (she was able to struggle violently even when held down by a considerable number of people); talking in languages of which she usually had no knowledge (Latin and Spanish, in her case); growling like an animal in a way that those present said would be very difficult to mimic; speaking in a changed voice (either low, growling and guttural or higher pitched than her usual voice); shunning holy objects, and responding with great antipathy towards anything religious. During the course of the exorcisms, and sometimes spontaneously at other times, Julia appeared to become the mouthpiece for various demons. She would go into a trance, and then changed voices would speak through her. The voices said things such as 'Leave her alone, you idiot,' 'She's ours,' 'Stop, you whores' (to the nuns), and simply 'Leave!' Most of what she said during the trances and later during exorcism was markedly antireligious. On coming to herself, she had no recollection of what she had said, or had been said through her.

As a psychiatrist, Gallagher was well aware that some of the symptoms described are a close match for the behaviour of patients with dissociative identity disorder (previously called multiple-personality disorder). As we have seen, there are very clear similarities between the symptoms of the disorder and the behaviour manifested by shamans deliberately channelling spirits and by individuals thought to be possessed against their will. Gallagher was, therefore, keen to point out the differences in his write-up of the case between Julia's state and the established psychopathology of dissociative identity disorder. These differences were paranormal activity and psychic ability.

Apparently, objects flew off shelves spontaneously and, most dramatically, she herself levitated, floating in the air for around 30 minutes during one of the exorcism rituals at a height of 15cm (6in). Both are forms of psychokinesis, which the laws of physics rule to be impossible. Psychokinesis has never been conclusively demonstrated, but if it were shown to exist, it could mean either that unexplained spiritual or psychic forces are at work or that the laws of physics as currently formulated are wrong or incomplete.

The other abilities which Julia appeared to

demonstrate are psychic. They involved her knowing details about people which she could not have known by normal methods, and about events at which she was not present and which she had not been told about. She was able to state the cause of death – the precise type of cancer – of a relative of a member of the team and commented to another of the team, whose cats had inexplicably started fighting at 2am, 'Those cats really went beserk last night, didn't they?' She was able to describe the physical setting, state of health and clothing of another member of the team who was away, as well as the décor of the room of a priest she had never met who was peripherally involved in the case. Indeed, she repeatedly demonstrated knowledge that she had no legitimate way of knowing. On one occasion her demonic voices interrupted a group phone conversation between team members when she was neither involved in the call nor aware of it. Several of those taking part heard the demonic voice saying the same types of thing that it said during her trances and exorcisms.

At the start of Julia's first exorcism session, the room became unaccountably cold even though it was a warm June day in New York. Once the process was underway and the voices emanating from Julia were being abusive and making strange noises, there was a change and the room became far too hot. Members of the team present sweated profusely and complained of unbearable heat coming from Julia.

The demons supposedly in Julia were able to distinguish holy water from unblessed water. If she was splashed with holy water, she would scream in pain, but if a priest surreptitiously switched to ordinary water, she was able to bear that with no discomfort.

Gallagher was not out to demonstrate whether or not exorcism works to dismiss spirits, and that is just as well since Julia called a halt to the sessions. Gallagher stated in his report, published in 2008, that she might yet take them up again but at the time of writing was still possessed. He was more interested in demonstrating, from the perspective of a psychiatric professional, that demonic possession is a genuine, though rare, state and different from mental illness. He concluded that often people are mistaken in identifying a state as possession when it is actually illness, but occasionally genuine possession is dismissed, either by healthcare professionals or priests, to the lasting harm of those who are suffering. For him, the point that marked Julia's case as one of genuine possession rather than dissociative identity disorder was the large element of preternatural knowledge and psychic ability.

This is broadly the position of most church officials who accept that possession occurs: that reported cases are more often than not instances of mental illness or dysfunction, but that, just rarely, there is genuine possession taking place. The current guidelines for the Catholic church involve extensive checks that the supposedly possessed person is not suffering from mental illness, and that unexplained phenomena (such as telekinesis or gnosis) have been independently witnessed before a case is considered for exorcism.

> 'We clearly felt, in this instance, that we were indeed dealing with a genuinely possessed individual, albeit one complicated even further by her Satanist history and 'psychic' abilities presumed consequent to her cultic involvement and/or her possessed state.'
>
> Richard E. Gallagher

THE EXORCIST – THE REAL STORY

The novel *The Exorcist* by William Blatty (1971) and the film of the book, released in 1973, give the most widely known accounts of an exorcism. Although presented as a fiction, the work was based on a real case. The child at the centre of the original story was a boy, referred to in records as Roland Doe. His real name has never been revealed. One of the priests involved in the case kept a full daily account of the progress of the exorcism, the most detailed modern account of an ancient ritual. Before his involvement, though, details are hazy. It's very difficult now to sort out the reliable from the unreliable information.

Born in Maryland in 1935, Roland was an only child who spent most of his time with adults and enjoyed the company of his aunt Harriet, who visited frequently. She was a Spiritualist, and introduced Roland to the Ouija board. When his aunt died, it seems that Roland might have tried to contact her using the board. According to some authorities, this would have made him vulnerable to assault by demonic forces.

Odd things began to happen in January 1949. Roland's grandmother heard a sound that seemed to be dripping water, but they could find no source. Soon

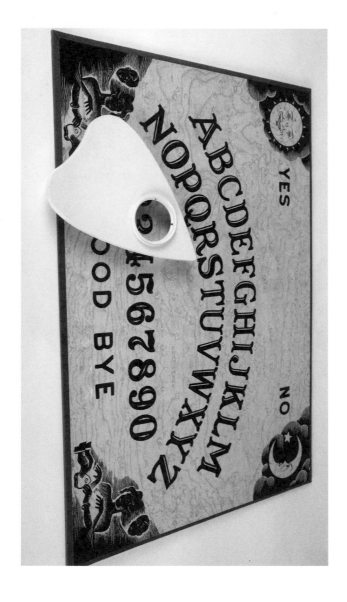

Linda Blair plays a victim of possession in a scene from the film The Exorcist, *1973.*

it was replaced by scratching, like claws on wood, which seemed to come from the floorboards under a bed. It was repeated every night, between about 7pm and midnight. Pest control inspectors found no evidence of rats or mice. Eleven nights after the scratching started, Aunt Harriet died; the scratching stopped. But soon it was replaced by a sound of persistent footsteps in Roland's room, as if someone in squeaky shoes were walking up and down beside his bed. Several nights later, his mother and grandmother lay in the room listening with him, but now the sounds were of feet marching to the beat of drums. This was supplemented with knocking sounds and then a wave of pressure that pushed the three of them against the bed. The bed began to shake, first gently and then violently. The scratching started up again, but now from inside the mattress.

> **OUIJA BOARDS**
> A Ouija board displays the alphabet and is used with a planchette – a small wheeled board – for communication with spirits. The users sit around, each putting a hand or finger on the planchette, while a spirit medium (or sometimes the whole company) questions the spirits. The planchette moves, spelling out the response one letter at a time.

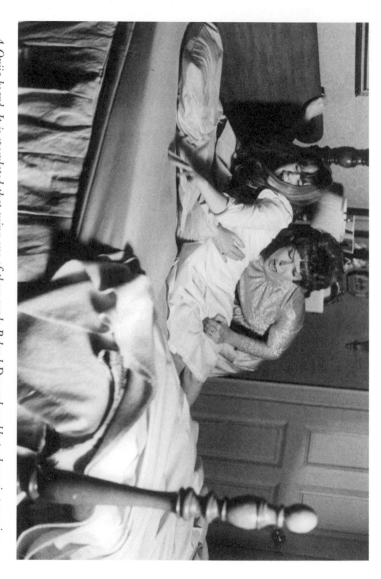

A Ouija board. It is speculated that using one of these made Roland Doe vulnerable to demonic possession.

Whatever was plaguing Roland's room seemed to follow him to school, as his desk would sometimes skitter across the room of its own accord. At home, objects would rise from a table, or throw themselves across a room, when he was nearby. Relatives saw a heavy chair tip him suddenly onto the floor, a Bible fly from a bookcase and land at his feet, a table in the kitchen tip over, and a rocking chair he was in unaccountably spin like a top.

One night, Roland's parents were awakened by his screaming. They went into his room and saw a heavy dresser slide across the floor and block the door, then all the drawers spontaneously opened and closed. Roland had become increasingly withdrawn, but one night, while asleep, he berated his parents with shocking obscenities, using words they were surprised that he even knew.

There is no accurate chronology of these early events, just fragments pieced together later by witnesses. Roland's parents tried several avenues for help, including a doctor, psychiatrist, psychic and their local Lutheran minister, Luther Miles Schulze, who was distinctly sceptical but kept his doubts to himself. He took the boy to his own home for a night for observation, expecting nothing to happen. He slept in the same room as the boy – but not for long. Soon, Roland's bed began to shake. The minister got him up and they had some cocoa, but the heavy chair on which Roland sat very slowly tipped over on its own. He set the boy to sleep on a pile of blankets on the floor, but he and the blankets glided over the floor, disappearing under a bed where Roland bounced up and down, lacerating his face on the springs on the underside of the bed. He seemed to be in a trance and did not flinch at the injuries.

Schulze was out of his depth. He came to accept that demonic possession must, after all, be a possibility. Roland was subdued during the day, but tormented all night. The scratching in the mattress continued, and soon scratch wounds began to appear on his body – long, shallow scratches like those made by a cat. Some of them seemed to form letters. Schulze recommended that the family consult a Catholic priest, as 'the Catholics know about things like this'.

Roland's father turned to Father E. Albert Hughes, a young priest with no previous experience of exorcism. At first he provided holy water to sprinkle around the boy's room and holy candles to light in it, but something picked up the bottle of holy water and smashed it, and when Roland's mother lit the candle the flame leapt up to the ceiling and threatened to burn the house down, so she had to put it out. With no options left, the bishop gave permission for an exorcism, and Roland was put in the care of Jesuit brothers at Georgetown

University Hospital. By this time, he was no longer attending school and was tormented nightly, waking with unexplained wounds.

The Mother Superior of the attending nuns insisted there should be no record of the exorcism, so all we know of it comes from second- and third-hand unofficial accounts. One states that when Father Hughes entered the room, Roland demanded that he remove a cross he was wearing, even though it was hidden under his clothes. Part way into the exorcism ritual, Roland managed to free one arm from his restraints. He reached under the bed and ripped out a bedspring, then attacked Father Hughes with it, slashing his arm viciously from wrist to elbow. The exorcism had to stop. Father Hughes had his wound stitched, and Roland was sent home, his condition no better.

Roland's parents discussed going to St Louis, where they had relatives, for a while. Then one night, as Roland got ready for bed, he looked in the bathroom mirror and screamed. The word 'Louis' had appeared in bleeding scratches across his chest. His mother, panicked, assured him that they would go to St Louis as soon as it could be arranged. Moaning, he pulled down his pyjamas to reveal 'Saturday' scratched into his skin. When his mother asked how long he wanted to go for, he screamed again and '3½ weeks' was scratched into his chest, as if from the inside.

The wisdom of going where the demons suggested might be doubted, but that's what they did. At first, Roland seemed better in St Louis. But when his mother suggested he start school there, the message 'No school' appeared scratched into his chest. Similar messages appeared whenever she mentioned it. The next port of call for the family was the local Jesuits. Their case was taken on by Father Raymond Bishop, who was quickly persuaded that something akin to possession was taking place. He enlisted the help of Father William Bowdern. The two priests tried to protect Roland by pinning holy relics to his bedclothes and sprinkling holy water in his room, but to no avail. There seemed to be no option but exorcism. They applied to the bishop of St Louis and he appointed Bowdern the exorcist. Bowdern was not pleased.

Bowdern and Bishop, assisted by a strong young Jesuit, Walt Halloran, started the exorcism on 16 March. Bowdern began with prayers, during which time the bed shook as before. When he began the exorcism itself, Roland screamed. As he proceeded, the boy continued to scream and writhe, red welts appearing across his body. Bishop described them as 'marks raised up above the surface of the skin, similar to an engraving'. It got worse. Lines of blood appeared across his legs, stomach and back, and then across his throat. Then letters traced themselves in scratches over his body – first HELL and, when Bowdern asked when the demon would leave, GO and X, which he took to mean the devil would leave either at 10am or in ten days' time. Roland fell asleep.

Bishop counted at least 25 marks on Roland's body. While Bowdern said a calming prayer, the boy struggled, punching his pillow and the headboard. He woke when Bowdern sprinkled holy water over him and said that he had been dreaming he fought a great slimy red devil, but that he felt so strong he might defeat it. They continued with the exorcism. Roland struggled, thrashing and writhing on the bed. Halloran and Roland's uncle, one at each shoulder, fought to hold him down while Roland spat at them and at Bowdern repeatedly. The ordeal went on hour after hour. At the very end, when Bowdern said the final prayers, Roland seemed to be in a peaceful sleep. It was deceptive. Soon, he started singing loudly, cackling and flailing as he sang first 'Way Down Upon the Swanee River' and then 'Old Man River.' Bowdern, though exhausted, prayed again. At 7:30 in the morning, Roland fell asleep.

The Jesuits were back the next night, and the night after, to face the same pattern of frenzied struggling, superhuman strength, and with only brief moments of respite. On the third night, Roland leapt to his feet and chanted 'Our Lady of Fatima, pray for us,' and soon after gestured as though he would vomit and then cried out, 'He's going! He's going! There he goes!' Soon after, he got out of bed, put on his bathrobe, chatted to the priests and then went to bed. Everyone was jubilant, and went to well-earned rest. But in just a few hours, Bowdern received a call – the demon was back.

The next night was even worse. Roland barked and snapped like a dog. When Bowdern demanded a sign from the demon, Roland urinated, on and on, so that foul-smelling urine soaked the bed. The boy complained of burning, in his throat and in his penis. The following night, there was more urine, and foul-smelling wind. Roland shouted abuse and blasphemies at the Jesuits, some so offensive that Bishop, who was keeping a diary of events, felt unable to record them.

It was getting too much for the family. Bowdern had Roland moved to the Alexian Brothers' Hospital for a night in a secure room to give them respite. It was a relatively peaceful night, and Bowdern felt optimistic for the future. He gained permission to prepare Roland for conversion to Catholicism, which he hoped would strengthen the boy spiritually, and moved him into his rectory. The next exorcism session was the worst so far. Roland broke Halloran's nose, and punched the nose of a new priest. He was abusive, urinated, broke wind, masturbated and taunted Bowdern, saying that he could see him in Hell in 1957.

On the tenth day, when Bowdern expected Roland to be free of the demon if he had interpreted the 'X' symbol correctly, the boy was calm. He remained so for four days, and Bowdern began to hope that the end was in sight. It wasn't. This time, Roland demanded a pencil. He covered a bed sheet and large leaves of paper with scribble that Bowdern struggled to decipher. It seemed to include threats against some of the clergy and cryptic messages about how long the possession would continue.

Bowdern accelerated Roland's baptism, hoping that this would give him extra strength against the powers of evil, but it seemed instead to intensify the battle. On the way to the baptism ceremony, Roland seized the steering wheel of the car, crashed the vehicle into a lamppost, grabbed his mother around the throat, and eventually had to be held down on the back seat while his aunt drove the final stretch. On their arrival at the church, Bowdern realized his plans for a proper baptism were not going to work. Instead of taking Roland into the church, they dragged him into the rectory where, over a period of four hours, Bowdern exploited Roland's brief moments of lucidity to complete the ceremony.

Far from making him easier to manage, baptism

seemed to make Roland's fury much worse. The next day, he raged for 15 hours, though usually he was calm during the daytime. Bowdern hurried through the necessary preparations for Roland's first communion, which was as much a struggle as the baptism had been. The latest scratches to appear on his body linked the number '18' with the demon's departure. Easter Sunday was 17 April; '18' didn't make sense to Bowdern.

For the first time, Roland showed awareness during the conscious spells of his lapses. He begged his father to take him home, saying he feared he was going crazy. Bowdern accompanied them to Maryland, where he struggled to find somewhere to continue the exorcism. The priest previously injured, Father Hughes, understandly did not want to be involved again. As Bowdern spoke the words of the prayers, and particularly 'Maria' and 'Jesu', the boy writhed in pain, shrieked and spat copious volumes of saliva with perfect aim, even though his eyes were closed. New wounds and scratches erupted all over his body. Some resolved into numbers: 4, 8, 10 and 16. Others formed words: HELL and SPITE. And at last he spoke in a hideous voice, saying, 'I will not go until a certain word is pronounced, and this boy will never say it.' A plan to bring the Host so that Roland could take communion had to be abandoned: although he had his eyes closed, he detected its presence and responded violently. Bowdern realized there was no option but to return to St Louis, as nowhere else would accommodate them for exorcism.

Back in the Alexian Hospital, the first night's exorcism was relatively calm, but during the second night, the word EXIT appeared in several places on Roland's body, written in bloody scratches. An arrow drawn down his chest and stomach pointed to his penis.

> 'His shirt was off. I saw those markings, and there was no way in the world he could have done it with a needle or his fingernails or anything else. Not with us watching him. They would just appear. At times he would have meaningless welts all over him. The kind you would get from a thorn. That sort of thing. Very, very red. I looked at them one time and they weren't there, and then the next time I looked at them, they were. Maybe ten seconds or fifteen seconds.'
>
> Walter Halloran

Bowdern tried to give Roland communion, struggling against the writhing, shrieking, spitting boy, who at one point punched him in the testicles. The holy words sent Roland into furious paroxysms. Bowdern could not get the particle of host to his lips, but struggled instead to give him spiritual communion (when the participant just has to say that they wish to receive communion). Between outbursts of cursing and screaming, Roland managed to say 'I want to receive you in Holy—' but could not say the word 'Communion'.

While there had once been a clear distinction between Roland's unconscious and lucid states, with the demons clearly in control during his unconscious moments, the boundaries of control now shifted. In a chilling display of power, the demonic voice began to predict (or dictate) what Roland would do in lucid moments. On one occasion, it said, 'I will make him wake up and demand a knife,' whereupon Roland opened his eyes, apparently lucid, and asked for a knife with which to cut his Easter egg. Bowdern could no longer trust even the lucid Roland.

The days over Easter were a struggle. Roland became ever more violent and was fiercely aggressive even in the middle of the day. Bowdern struggled to work out what he should make of the word that the demon would not allow Roland to say and of the numbers that had been scratched into Roland's skin, particularly of '18'. During his few lucid moments, Roland would struggle to ask for communion. Bowdern hung holy medals around the boy's neck and prevented him removing them even when he complained that they burned him.

Bowdern changed his tactic and used a calmer, quieter voice for the prayers, no longer commanding the demon in a loud and stern voice. And then, at 10:45 pm on 18 April, Roland spoke in a new voice:

'Satan! Satan! I am Saint Michael, and I command you, Satan, and the other evil spirits to leave the body in the name of *Dominus*. Immediately! Now! NOW! NOW!'

For a few minutes, Roland suffered the most violent of contortions and screamed, then said calmly, 'He's gone!' It was over. But still Bowdern did not dare to relax and believe what he heard. He had learned that the demon could be a surprisingly convincing deceiver. But the next day a loud, resounding boom echoed through the entire hospital. That was the sign that the old accounts of exorcisms had told him to expect. As the noise died away, Bowdern knew that Roland really was free at last.

> 'I can assure you of one thing: the case in which I was involved was the real thing. I had no doubt about it then and I have no doubt about it now.'
>
> Father Bowdern

Roland Doe afterwards lived a peaceful life, growing up to marry, raise children and work for NASA before retiring to live in Washington, DC. He is still alive at the time of writing.

The suburbs of Prince George's County, Maryland, USA. The possession and subsequent exorcism of Roland Doe would have unfolded in a neighbourhood such as this in Cottage City, Prince George's County, MD.

BEGONE SATAN!

One of the most famous cases of demonic possession from the USA concerns Anna Ecklund from Earling, Iowa. Her final exorcism is recorded in a short pamphlet, *Begone Satan!*, which exists in several versions. Anna is also known as 'Mary X'.

Born in 1882, Anna was apparently possessed by the age of 14, when she displayed a strong aversion to anything holy. She could not bear to enter a church, feeling a strong force preventing her from going in, and displayed an obsessive interest in disturbing sexual acts. By the time she was 26, she was considered thoroughly possessed. At this point, a Capuchin monk called Father Theophilus Riesinger carried out an exorcism. The exorcism seemed successful, but Anna became possessed again. It was claimed that the possession came about because Anna's father and his mistress, Mina, cursed the spices put into her food, and – as Mina was said to be a practising witch – invited devils to take possession of her.

In 1928, when Anna was 46 years old, Father Theophilus began again, assisted by Father Steiger. This time, he first moved Anna to a convent run by Franciscan nuns. It was the custom of the nuns to bless all food consumed there. Anna did not know this, but immediately refused the food offered her, hissing like a cat when the nuns placed blessed food in front of her. The kitchen had to prepare unblessed food for her as she would immediately recognize and reject anything else.

The exorcism began with Anna lying on a mattress on an old iron bed and held down by six strong nuns. Her clothes were tightly bound to prevent her stripping them off. As soon as the ritual began, Anna clamped her mouth shut and fell unconscious. Over the coming days, she exhibited many of the features familiar from earlier accounts of possession.

She displayed inhuman strength, so that right from the start the six nuns could not hold her down. Most alarmingly, she sprang from the bed to cling to the wall above the door where she crouched, somehow holding onto the wall with her fingers. It took great effort to drag her back down. In her unconscious state, she blasphemed and abused everyone present, not in her own voice but in a changed voice that came from deep in her throat while her lips did not move. She spoke languages she did not know, and revealed secrets that she could not have been privy to, including sins committed in childhood by the nuns and priests around her. She vomited, urinated, defecated, drooled and spat, producing prodigious amounts of fluid and solid waste even though she was barely eating or drinking.

She took only small quantities of milk and water, nearly starving to death over the course of the exorcism, yet she – like Roland Doe – could produce improbably great streams of urine. Her vomit included tobacco leaves and other plant debris. A hideous stench often appeared, and clouds mosquitoes and other flies would appear and then disappear.

But there were even more dramatic physical signs. Sometimes her head swelled grossly or grew elongated, her face lost its ghostly pallor and glowed bright red, or her eyes bulged from their sockets. Sometimes her lips grew to be the size of hands. Her body bloated to the point where it was double its normal size and seemed that it should burst, but then deflated and became so rigid and heavy that the iron bed bent under her weight (a phenomenon known as 'paranormal gravity').

Beelzebub seemed to be the principal demon. He revealed that he had been sent to Anna by her father. Jacob had, he said, tried to force Anna into incestuous sex while he was alive and was punishing her now for her resistance. Mina, too, was present, and was as spiteful and blasphemous as any of the demons. She had been damned for her adulterous relationship with Jacob and for the murder of four children – which might have meant that she had four abortions, rather than serial infanticide. The spirit of Judas Iscariot, who betrayed Jesus and later hanged himself, was tormenting her with the aim of getting her to kill herself and so be sent to Hell.

The most unusual feature, though, was that the priests had a vivid, waking vision of devils. For the last half-hour of the exorcism, Father Theophilus saw Lucifer and Beelzebub trapped in a corner of the room. The room was filled with flames. Lucifer was extremely tall, with hooves and matted black fur on his lower body. He wore a crown and was furious with Father Theophilus because he could not harm him. Beelzebub was also present.

The exorcism lasted 23 days, divided into three sessions between 18 August and 23 December. The sessions were often interrupted by bouts of howling and screaming that only gradually subsided under constant prayer. Sometimes extra, minor demons interrupted proceedings and caused Anna's face to become hideously and unrecognizably distorted.

'Her whole body became so horribly disfigured that the regular contour of her body vanished. Her pale, deathlike and emaciated head, often assuming the size of an inverted water pitcher, became as red as glowing embers. Her eyes protruded out of their sockets, her lips swelled up to proportions equalling the size of hands, and her thin emaciated body was bloated to such

> enormous size that the pastor and some of the
> Sisters drew back out of fright, thinking that the
> woman would be torn to pieces and burst asunder.
> At times her abdominal region and extremities
> became as hard as iron and stone. In such instances
> the weight of her body pressed into the iron
> bedstead so that the iron rods of the bed bent to
> the floor.'
>
> *Begone, Satan!* by Reverend Carl Vogl,
> translated by Reverend Celestine Kapsner

On the final day, 23 December, Anna suddenly stood
upright on her bed; it looked as if she might levitate
again. Father Theophilus blessed her and called out,
'Depart ye fiends of hell! Begone Satan, the Lion of
Judah reigns!' Anna fell back onto the bed, and the
shouts of departing demons came from her: 'Beelzebub,
Judas, Jacob, Mina. Hell, hell, hell.' An unbearable
odour filled the room, the last sign of the defeated
demons, as Anna opened her eyes and smiled. Then,
with tears of joy streaming down her face, she praised
Jesus for her deliverance.

CLARA GERMANA CELE, SNAKE GIRL

It's relatively unusual for a victim of possession to seek out exorcism on their own, yet that is what Clara Germana Cele did in 1906. A 16-year-old black South African, she was a student at the Mariannhill St Michael's Mission School in Umzinto when she visited Father Erasmus Hörner for confession. Orphaned in infancy, she had been at the school since the age of four. Her confession was unusual – she told Father Hörner that she had made a pact with the Devil. Over the coming weeks, her behaviour became increasingly odd. On 20 August, in between growling like an animal, tearing at her clothes and apparently talking to invisible beings, she implored one of the sisters to call Father Hörner so that she could make a full confession. 'But quick, quick, or Satan will kill me. He has me in his power!' And later: 'You have betrayed me. You have promised me days of glory, but now you treat me cruelly.'

Clara's behaviour was reported by the nuns at Mariannhill. Her skin burned if she was sprinkled with holy water, she lashed out violently whenever sacred objects were nearby, even if they were hidden from view, and she knew details about the personal lives of others that she had no legitimate way of knowing. When she became violent, she seemed to have immense and improbable strength, easily overpowering the adults who tried to hold her down. She could apparently speak and understand several languages she had never learned, including French, German and Polish.

More alarmingly for the nuns, Clara could – and regularly did – levitate up to 1.5m (5ft) from the floor, her clothes sticking to her body, so her skirts did not spread outwards around her. Only sprinkling holy water over her could bring her back down to earth. The water brought a short-lived recovery from the possessed state. All this is fairly routine for those claimed to be possessed, but Clara added an extra dimension. She was said to be able to change into a snake-like creature and move sinuously across the floor, her body as flexible as rubber. When she once bit a nun on the arm, the bite mark was reported as looking like the twin puncture wounds of a snake bite.

> 'No animal had ever made such sounds. Neither the lions of East Africa not the angry bulls. At times, it sounded like a veritable herd of wild beasts, orchestrated by Satan, had formed a hellish choir.'
> Attending nun at the mission

Father Hörner, with the help of another priest, Reverend Mansueti, carried out an exorcism on Clara on 11 September 1906. It lasted most of the day and long into the night. During the exorcism, she attempted to strangle one of the priests with his stole. The ritual was repeated the next morning, when the demon leaving her said he would signal his departure by an act of levitation. Clara's body duly rose from the ground in the chapel in front of 170 witnesses. She was declared free of the influence of the Devil.

But that wasn't the end of it. In January of the next year, Clara – evidently not a girl to learn from her mistakes – claimed to have made another pact with the Devil. Again, a two-day exorcism was needed to release her. This time, the demon's departure was marked by an overpowering stench, reported by witnesses. No more is known about Clara Germana Cele or her later life, but it seems she stopped making pacts with the Devil, at least.

MICHAEL TAYLOR

The small town of Ossett in northern England seems an unlikely place for a demonically inspired murder, yet that is what Michael Taylor claimed in 1974. Taylor and his wife, Christine, lived there with their five children. They were Christian, but not devout and not church-goers, until a friend introduced them to the Christian Fellowship, a group led by 22-year-old Marie Robinson.

After the couple attended their first service, the group held a meeting at their house. When one woman present began to cry, Marie Robinson responded by shaking, which she later explained: 'I started shaking, which in me usually means that the Holy Spirit is very active, and His power is ready to be used in one direction. I felt, if only this power was for Mike, because I knew he had a bad back and was depressed because he could not get a job.' She (unaccountably) decided to exorcise the weeping woman and knelt in front of her, praying in tongues. Taylor also began to speak in tongues.

Over the next 12 days, Taylor seemed to develop an infatuation with Marie Robinson. One night, they stayed up together making the sign of the cross over one another and fearing the effect of the full moon.

On another occasion, they kissed, but then broke apart. Robinson declared that it was wrong, and that Taylor loved his wife. Christine, not unreasonably, suspected that there was something going on between them.

The pair gave an odd account to police later of how this apparently simple state of attraction in a religious setting quickly degenerated into something distinctly unnatural. Taylor's version was that 'she seduced me with her eyes. I can still see those eyes. I saw her standing naked before me, and I was naked...' Robinson was the one who introduced the demonic element: 'I suddenly glanced at Mike and his whole features changed. He looked almost bestial. He kept looking at me and there was a really wild look in his eyes. I started screaming at him out of fear. I started speaking in tongues. Mike also screamed at me in tongues . . . I was on the verge of death and I seemed to come to my senses. I knew that only the name of Jesus would save me and I just started saying over and over again 'Jesus'. When Chris [Mike's wife] heard me calling on the name of Jesus she started saying it too, and I believe firmly that it was only by calling on His name that I was not killed.'

At the next meeting, Mike Taylor was given absolution for this outburst, but he continued to act oddly. His behaviour was enough to persuade the Christian Fellowship that he was possessed by demons.

They encouraged Mike and Christine to attend St Thomas's Church in Gawber at midnight on 5 October 1974 for an exorcism. The exorcism was carried out by the vicar, Reverend Peter Vincent, his wife Sally, a Methodist minister named Reverend Smith and his wife Margaret, a Methodist lay preacher and a member of the Fellowship group.

The exorcism took nearly eight hours. Taylor was restrained and laid on hassocks (cushions used for kneeling on the floor during prayers). The lawyer defending Taylor, Harry Ognall QC, described it in court as 'grotesque and wicked malpractice posing in the guise of religion'. They forced Taylor to confess to sins he had not committed, pushed a crucifix into his mouth and sprinkled him with holy water. They set fire to a wooden cross which he was wearing. They listed the 'demons' that they cast out of him – around 40 in all – including 'incest', 'bestiality', 'blasphemy', 'lewdness', 'heresy' and 'masochism'. At 7am, the group declared that three spirits remained in him: 'violence', 'anger', and 'murder'. Margaret Smith claimed to have received 'word from the Lord that the spirit of murder was going to break out'. She specifically referred to Christine Taylor in this context. Even so, this group of people who believed so firmly in the existence of these demons decided to stop at 8am because everyone was tired. They sent

Taylor home, with the demons of murder, violence and anger still not expelled and – it would seem – roused by the exorcism.

At 10am, Taylor was found by police walking naked along a road and covered with blood. When asked whose blood it was, he replied, 'It is the blood of Satan.' But it was the blood of his wife. He had killed her with his bare hands, and torn her apart. He gouged out her eyes, ripped out her tongue and all but removed her face.

Taylor was found not guilty of Christine's murder on grounds of insanity, and the cause of her death was recorded as 'misadventure'. After four years in secure psychiatric units, the first two of them in Broadmoor, Taylor was released. He was later charged with the indecent assault of a teenage girl and – having no previous convictions – was given a community rehabilitation order.

The clerics involved in the exorcism were unrepentant. The defending barrister blamed them for the murder of Christine, saying that without the exorcism the crime would never have happened. Their response was that the murder simply proved that they had been right about Taylor and he really was possessed by demons. If that were the case, they were surely negligent in letting him go home with the demon responsible for murder still resident in him and stirred up for action. But Reverend Vincent responded to criticism with an assurance that God knows what he's doing: 'I am quite convinced God will bring good out of this in His own way, however tragic it was at the time.'

'Let those who truly are responsible for this killing stand up. We submit that Taylor is a mere cipher. The real guilt lies elsewhere. Religion is the key. Those who have been referred to in evidence, and those clerics in particular, should be with him in spirit now in this building and each day he is incarcerated in Broadmoor, and not least on the day he must endure the bitter reunion with his five motherless children.'

Harry Orgnall, QC, at Taylor's trial

Conclusion

The tales of possession presented here are only a tiny fraction of those recorded, and more are reported every year. They come from the United States, South America, the Philippines, Japan, and parts of Europe and Africa. Until the 1970s, the United States saw very few claimed cases of possession, but they have soared in recent decades. Yet an increase in claims has brought us no closer to understanding what is going on.

Whether we wish to see possession as a form of mental illness or infestation by demonic beings, it seems to be true in all times and cultures that a person becomes 'possessed' when they believe they will (when cursed, when persuaded they are possessed) and is freed from possession when they believe they will be freed (through some ritual or exorcism, or through accepting a community's verdict that they are not possessed). For this reason, exorcism rituals in all times and places are characterized by commanding the possessing spirits to leave, and often issuing threats against them, alongside prayers or invocations to a god or benign spirit.

EXORCISM – A DOUBLE-EDGED SWORD

Many of the cases we have seen here show the exorcist suffering immense difficulties in his attempts to rid the possessed individual of their demons. Many exorcists have also fallen prey to possession themselves through the process. The entire mythology stresses the ease with which people can 'catch' demons, and the many instances of group possession or hysteria corroborate that view. Exorcism, by necessity, involves endorsing the belief that the person is possessed. So in confirming the belief, the exorcist makes the condition all the more entrenched. First you thought you might be possessed and now someone tells you that you actually are possessed. It is very difficult to treat possession successfully, so the person who believes they are possessed is likely to slump further into despair, further beyond the reach of help, the more the idea of possession is entertained and reinforced. It is a vicious circle. In the case of Michael Taylor, who brutally murdered his wife after an exorcism, it appears that murder was suggested to him by the exorcist, and that he might never have harmed his wife if this idea had not been implanted and nurtured along with the conviction that he was possessed.

Since at least the late 19th century, some people have interpreted demonic possession as a type of neurosis or psychological disorder. It helps to name and classify, but it does little to explain. If we say there is somehow a second human personality or identity within the mind of the afflicted person, that still does not tell us very much. We have no idea how a person's primary identity of personality – the manifestation of 'mind' – comes about or operates, so adding a second similarly mysterious entity is hardly discovering a vein of clarity. It gives us language with which to discuss and model what we see, but brings us no closer to knowing why or how it happens than if we talk of demons taking over the spirit or mind.

The only thing that is clear is that phenomena of the type labelled demonic possession have happened for as long as humans have been able to record them. It would seem reasonable to believe that something actually happens that causes people (or spirits) to behave (or interact) in these ways – we just don't know what it is. Perhaps the last word should go to Richard Lloyd Parry, who documented the possession of tsunami survivors: 'It doesn't really matter whether you believe in ghosts. What's real is the suffering and the pain.'

An exorcism performed by Hermes Cifuentes in La Cumbre, Colombia in 2012 on a woman known as Diana R., who claimed to have been possessed by evil spirits.

21ST-CENTURY EXORCISM

Exorcism is as popular as ever in some parts of the world. Brother Hermes – Hermes Cifuentes – is a priest in Columbia who claims to have carried out more than 35,000 exorcisms over 25 years. He begins by plastering his subjects with black mud, then performs a ritual which sees them blindfolded and staked to the ground, surrounded by eggs, limes and crucifixes within a protective circle of fire. As Brother Hermes coaxes or drives 'demons' from his possessed subjects, the spirits often put up a struggle. His treatment seems successful – he is highly sought-after, despite the charge of US $35 for a diagnosis and $230 for a full exorcism.

Index

PICTURE CREDITS